TEACHING TIPS for HorseBACK RIDING INSTRUCTORS

by

Jo Struby

RoseDog 🐾 Books

PITTSBURGH, PENNSYLVANIA 15222

RoseDog Books
701 Smithfield Street
Pittsburgh, PA 15222
Visit our website at *www.rosedogbookstore.com*

ISBN: 978-1-4809-0034-9
eISBN: 978-1-4809-0094-3

TEACHING TIPS for HorseBACK RIDING INSTRUCTORS

A Chronicle Collection of 61 Teaching Topics

for Instructors of *Horse*back Riding

by

Jo Struby

*To the horses that have been my long-term personal mounts;
all contributed greatly
to my education and thus, to the education of my students.*

*Susie & Friskie, I owe these ponies my start with equines
Hoyle Bars, my first "pony" who really was a horse
Honeycomb, also a tall pony who allowed me to jump over
    5 feet at a young age, more than once
Annie J., my first horse, a n d my first Event mount
Malama, my first horse to train and resell
Vic Mambo, Thunder and Grape Ape, who collectively,
    showed me just how different horses can be
Hannah's Hollywood, we almost made it to our first
    Three Day Event
Ole Charter, both of us made it to our first Three Day
    Event, a n d much more
F'er Vesence, along side of Ole Charter enabled me to
    gain experience at the FEI levels of Dressage
Dulcinea, a mare of determination, trust earned and
    only t h e n, trust given back
Todo Regal King, a mighty quarter horse who went
    places in the Eventing world few of his breed have
Waldur Dewey, a tender heart who always gave all he had
H. Nicolaus, my best friend and first Advanced Level
    Event horse
Senetir, Senova and Kashman, shared many insights to
    the fine abilities of this light breed
Mr. Phoenix, a horse with the talent to impress Kings
    and Queens
Hungarian Jokepu, a bright hearted mare, who eagerly
    learns all she can and passes this wonderful virtue
    onto her foals*

W elcome to my Teaching Tips for Horseback Riding Instructors. With these tips, it has been my desire to share PEARLS OF WISDOM. Many references exist on the subject of riding horses and horsemanship, yet fewer references exist on specifically the subject of teaching horseback riding. The purpose of these teaching tips has been to provide a meaningful reference for our teachers who instruct horseback riding. Thus, these topics about instructors' concerns, have been chosen carefully and written over a period of time. Each topic stands by itself and is not dependent upon reading any of the topics afore.

Originally these tips on teaching topics were written monthly and sold by annual subscription during 1996 through 2000. During those years, my modest and loyal subscribers were very enthusiastic and appreciative of the support these teaching tips provided for their instruction of horseback riding. For this edition, all 61 topics have been combined into one resource and arranged into chapters of teaching curriculum. Furthermore, a detailed traditional index has been added to achieve a broader flexible use of all the subject matter.

As since their beginning in 1996, my teaching tips have been presented in both written and spoken word for the instructor. Today's purpose: to enable the instructor a personal comparison of two entirely different learning environments upon content. This unique opportunity provides an indispensable setting for the instructor of horseback riding. From these two different methods of instruction, written presentation and oral presentation, the instructor will personally experience two different learning environments, enabling the instructor as the learner, to identify and compare benefits and differences of both methods as they apply to the content at hand. Meanwhile, each instructor who diligently goes through this process with the majority of 61 topics, will also achieve those initial steps of evaluating the benefits and differences for future planning of instruction; similar and dissimilar. Primary goals for horsemanship curriculum planning include decisions upon when and when not to, apply more than one method of instruction. In limbo to this issue of singular or multiple methods of instruction for curriculum implementation is the end result for the learner. When do such decisions result in desirable synergistic advantages? Or when do such decisions result in undesirable curriculum overload and confusion?

Since my effort with this literary work has not been to produce a textbook but a resource and learning tool for the instructor of horseback riding, be advised to liberally use the index as well as the chapters' listing to find a subject you are seeking. Hopefully you will find it there or some other related subject that will advance your skills. Those new to teaching horseback riding will find useful suggestions and sound fundamentals in the pages to follow. However, the new horseback riding instructor will also need to combine this book with texts of curriculum content for the discipline/s and level/s they teach. Meanwhile, tenured instructors will undoubtedly enjoy this resource of teaching tips due to the easy-to-read short article style. For flexibility across the riding disciplines, the example teaching situations rotate between the various styles of riding. After all, the fundamentals of *teaching* horseback riding *are* the same. Knowing that lifestyles and learning preferences strongly dictate our time for acquiring or continuing our education as horseback riding instructors, it has been my goal to provide a versatile reference. After all, experience in the teaching arena is only part of our journey toward excellence. I hope this collection of teaching tips for *horse*back riding instructors will help *our* teachers, for many, many years to come.

E n j o y!

CHAPTERS

Chapter Five, INSTRUCTOR SKILLS

Chapter Six, INSTRUCTOR STRATEGIES

Chapter Seven, TEACHING TOOLS & TECHNIQUES

Chapter Eight, STUDENT SKILLS

Chapter Nine, STUDENT NEEDS & DESIRES

The Author's Side Note On Using This Reference:

This reference is not a substitute for instructor horsemanship and equestrian skills.

This reference is not a curriculum guide for instruction of a certain level of instruction.

This reference *IS* a set of short articles/essays designed to aid and support instructors of ALL equestrian disciplines in the art and science of teaching *horse*back riding.

The Author's spoken word recordings of these teaching tips topics can be obtained from the Author.

Chapter One

GENERAL PHILOSOPHY FOR INSTRUCTION

TIPS FOR TEACHING SAFETY IN YOUR RIDING LESSONS:

While safety practices by an instructor are fundamental; TEACHING your students *about* safety and *how* and *when* to apply practices that lead to safer equestrian activity, is our *end goal* as instructors. Lessons where safety dwindles after the initial tack check, does little but pay lip service to safety for riding. Students who rely on the instructor to keep things safe are penny wise pound foolish. Teaching our students to make safety decisions, empowers students to take responsibility for their safety which serves them both during and outside their lessons. What is safer? How can safety hazards be minimized? What are helpful caution signs? How can we discriminate appropriate safety practices for use during various riding conditions? And the list goes on. Lets look at four safety categories - listed in order of importance: *The Horse; Our Judgments; The Environment and Our Equipment.*

THE HORSE: Alois Podhajsky wrote in his book: <u>My Horses, My Teachers</u>: "..... It is of the four legged teachers that I want to speak, those who my interest in and devotion to the sport of riding made me learn to appreciate, to understand and to respect from my earliest childhood. This should not mean that all horses belong in the group of good teachers....." In terms of safety, some horses assist in helping things to be safer, while others escalate the danger factor. Most frequently, younger horses are in this latter category because of their "greeness", but Podhajsky also points out certain bloodlines in horses seem to be more challenging than others. When it comes to horse ownership, especially with green horse - green rider combinations, a great deal of romanticism is involved. Thus, at times, instructors and students try to make due with unsuitable horses. The current trend is to label unsuitability problems as "personality problems" (the horse's or student's) while the *true problem* is the horse is simply *unsuitable* for the rider. While there are workable resolutions aside from selling one's horse, all of these involve the rider riding a different horse.... at least for a while. Guiding your students to ride suitable horses means they will graduate in their skills with their confidence in tact. Encourage your students to treat their mount/s with respect; *endless learning comes from suitable horses.*

OUR JUDGMENTS: Guiding a situation to be safer is just the first step for riding instructors. Next, we need to teach our students how to make safer judgment calls *themselves*. This relies on increasing your students' knowledge. As we progress with our equestrian activities, we learn there are lots of safety *details*. Many safety rules of thumb take on *asterisk*. For example: One should always ride with a tight girth. True, but beyond the tolerant beginner school horse, this principal needs further interpretation: in order to be safest, a girth should be the appropriate *degree* of tightness which will keep the saddle in place considering the conformation *and* comfort of each particular horse while also considering the balance of the rider. Setting up "mock" situations, helps in teaching students to develop their safety judgment calls. A mock situation for proper girth tightness would be: as I lunge this round, mutton withered horse with only a slightly snug girth look at what happens to the saddle as compared to the last horse I lunged whom easily held the saddle on with his high withers and broad ribs. Next, look at how this sensitive, high withered, thin skinned horse dislikes a "too tight" a girth; .... and so on.

THE ENVIRONMENT: Our friends "the horse", are equipped with intricate herd and fight reactions. Even horses "imprinted" by humans at birth readily have these instincts. Due to this fact, consider the horse's environment to start with the other equines they are in the company of (or lack thereof), and secondly the world beyond (which includes us, other animals, the wind, the rain, tractors, a mirror and so on). Half of our challenge becomes manipulating the horse's environment in our favor for safety purposes. A frequently seen example of this is a beginner lesson when riders are put in a file. Susiebell is put at the back of the file *because* she argues with Trigger unless he is at the front of the file.

Additionally, because horses have *keen* senses, they also need to become "accustomed" to new environments. While a new environment might "wake up" an older school master, extremes of this factor can make a less experienced horse *unrideable*. Take care to gradually introduce changes in a horse's environment for the safety of all.

OUR EQUIPMENT: In today's world of gadgetry, we do not lack for equipment "options", yet *safe use* remains a large concern. Essential are: *equipment in good repair and condition* - tack, horse & rider clothing, footing, fencing, jumps etc; *equipment that fits* - expensive nor well kept equipment can protect a rider or aid in communicating with horses if it is adjusted incorrectly or *can't* be adjusted correctly. And last but not least - *the proper selection of equipment*. As William Steinkraus points out in an earlier (wonderful) article for the AHSA Horse Show magazine, "As long as I've been around horses, bitless bridles (hackamores) and the various forms of gags have been cyclically in and out of fashion, depending on whether some particular star rider was using them at the time." Fads, unfortunately, are not limited just to bits. The popularity of horse back protecting pads has not addressed when they are actually making matters worse; neoprene splint boots continue to be put on horses with sensitive skin, and so on. Equipment safety equals: good working condition, proper use & fit *and* comfort for horse and rider too!

TIPS FOR TEACHING HORSEMANSHIP:

Aside from teaching safety, probably the single most concern of horseback riding instructors is gaining ample opportunities to teach general horsemanship. Consider this definition of HORSEMANSHIP:

> A loving, knowledgeable and skillful association of man
> with horses, resulting in mutual goals and ambition.

So how can we *t e a c h* horsemanship? Certainly riding lessons provide some of our opportunities for *horsemanship* instruction; however, we also need to seek other opportunities. Contributing to our student's general horsemanship is an on-going process. Many valuable opportunities are often informal situations such as: working side by side with your student in the barn, encouraging horsemanship discussions while traveling to a horse show, asking your student to help with nursing a school horse's health problem, etc. Teaching horsemanship, more than any other area of instruction for equestrians, requires *our* leadership in the "role model" sense. Horsemanship is a way of life, rather than a particular skill to learn. Our strongest teachings will come from our own association with horses. Our plans, actions, and decisions, go a long way to set examples for students. Furthermore, the staff of a barn, plays almost an equal role in teaching horsemanship. Barn managers, stall cleaners, horse handlers, even weekend help, do influence horsemanship education. Here are some specific ideas for *teaching* horsemanship.

FOR THE NOVICE, STRUCTURE YOUR PROGRAM TO INCLUDE EDUCATION ON HORSEMANSHIP. Equestrian newcomers, often romanced by riding a horse, fail to understand the value or meaning of horsemanship. Make horsemanship a *part* of the novice's program. This can be achieved in numerous ways. Several examples are: every fourth lesson in your program is an unmounted lesson where general horsemanship curriculum is covered. Rainy day lessons are held and devoted to horsemanship topics of the *student's* choice. Scheduled in advance and announced: once a month, invite your students to watch you perform routine horse care for an hour. A formal demonstration or simply your students joining you to watch the proper cleaning of a stall, feeding, clipping, bathing, treating a wound, or handling a foal will go a long way to teach horsemanship.

EVALUATE HORSEMANSHIP KNOWLEDGE AND SKILLS OF THE EXPERIENCED EQUESTRIANS WHOM ARE BEGINNING LESSONS WITH YOU. Oddly enough, experienced equestrians are not always well versed horsemen. Furthermore, when horsemanship is lacking, frequently, "mechanical" riders result. These riders lack unity with the horse, though they possess the technical skills of riding. Focus on evaluating their skills - be careful not to "test" their knowledge and skills at this time. Some ideas for providing an *evaluation* of horsemanship knowledge and skills are: Pair this equestrian with one of your students of the same riding level whom you know to have the horsemanship capabilities usual for this level of riding. Identify horsemanship tasks for them to accomplish together such as: putting a bridle back together or putting splint boots on a horse soon to be turned out. In addition to evaluating the quality of the their task performed, ask them if they learned any tips from each other. Their answers will help you with your evaluation. If a rider brings their own horse to the lesson, make the time to watch their *preparations* for their lesson. How do they handle their horse? How do they tack the horse up and how do they respond if a problem arises? These insights gained, will go a long way to help you in evaluating new students' horsemanship skills.

UTILIZE ESTABLISHED RIDING SCHOOLS, FOR MAINTAINING HIGH STANDARDS OF HORSEMANSHIP. While newer establishments are all too often subjected to business pressures of survival, established riding schools provide foundation cornerstones of high standards for horsemanship. These establishments offer to *ALL* horsemen, a camaraderie. Therefore, a field trip for staff, students or both, can help to elevate your barn's standards. Such an activity is fun and encourages higher standards at home. The occasion might be an open house the facility is offering, a seminar or clinic, or an individual arrangement you have made. Rub elbows with barns you respect!

TIPS FOR DEVELOPING NATURAL RIDERS:

The word "natural" has been of household popularity during the latter part of last century; yet we struggle or disagree on what *IS* natural. Surely, any instructor enjoys having a student who is "a natural" but does that mean *any* difficulty negates inclusion into this special club? If so, no one could teach a natural rider anything ...... as that "natural" rider already knows, already can do, etc. Do you know any "natural" riders like this?

Also popular, is the concept of learning to ride "naturally." Yet, many different conditions and environments have been proposed as "more natural for learning" horseback riding. More and more recipes on how to "best" teach horseback riding are surfacing. For sure, the posture that there are approaches "more natural" which instructors *should* apply, is a debate that seems to be just warming up. Perhaps this is because during the last century, the science of horseback riding instruction has taken on the recreational and leisure world; very different from the primary transportation and labor roles of equines for humans of years ago; at least, in first world countries.

Consider all reasonable ideas devoted to *developing natural riders*. There is a solid agreement among physical educators that sport skills are learned through physical and mental practice; thus "naturalized." Researchers declare the concept of an all-round star athlete to be a rare occurrence if not a myth. This is because the physical requirements of individual sports such as balancing and coordination are unique to *each* sport, thus are learned best by doing that sport. According to sports researcher R.H. Dave, the definition of a naturalized skill is: *one or more skills, that can be performed with ease and are automatic with limited physical and mental exertion*. So, a natural rider, for most people, is a rider who has "mastered" riding skills.

In the riding ring, to *develop* natural riders, we must provide lessons that will progress a rider's education toward this goal. Secondly, how much physical and mental ware-with-all each student brings to this equation influences our lesson plans and the possibilities. Furthermore, not all riders want to achieve naturalized skills to the heights of the athletic scales. Seeking a widely accepted definition of what a "natural rider" *IS*, would be a challenge. Instead, lets look at some fundamental elements *we* can apply in the riding ring to help our students develop "naturalized" riding skills:

- *Consider and provide for safety*
- *Arrange the environment for learning*
- *Develop confidence building lesson plans*
- *Present individual lessons which build skills*
- *Link all individual lessons toward common goals*
- *Allow for sufficient practice time to develop the skill/s*
- *Allow for trial and error, experimentation and discovery*
- *Provide measures of achievement the student understands*

What the instructor does and what a lesson "looks" like, can be vastly different but equally suitable depending on your student/s and your method / preferences of instruction. For example, several fearless eight year olds on suitable ponies, receiving a lesson on how to post in a 40' x 40' ring, will *look* very different from several adults, also fearless, also learning to post, on suitable medium size horses being lead one at a time in a much larger space. Both groups of students are being provided a sound approach for learning posting. Why similar lessons (to be learned) *look* different (in how they are taught), is largely due to students' needs, instructor's preferences and the horses.

Teaching recipes are *needed* for new riding instructors - they provide a system and structure. Experienced instructors always benefit from studying and applying recipes that differ from their own; new ideas and experiences are gained. Head instructors of riding schools cultivate "school recipes." Free lance instructors develop their own "personal recipe." While an individual instructor might have more freedom, they have no less responsibility. *Developing* natural riders boils down to cultivating naturalized riding skills!

Chapter Two

OUR CO-TEACHERS, THE HORSE

TIPS FOR LETTING THE HORSES HELP YOU TEACH:

Instructors who guide their students to learn from their horses, teach *horsemanship* not just *riding skills*. In many respects, horses are much like us. They have good days and bad days; they learn from their mistakes; they have social concerns; they proceed in their learning as they age. And, they have a great capacity to teach. When a seasoned school horse steps under a falling student, this is not just by chance. Most horses are very capable of numerous supports to our lessons if we respect and utilize what they have to offer. Contributions from our equine teaching partners can keep us from talking until we are blue in the face while bolstering more harmonious riding skills.

READING THE HORSE'S BODY LANGUAGE. While "equus" has body language natural to its species, in addition, horses develop body language specific to *being* ridden. Examples of *problem* body language are: ticklish to the rider's lower leg causing tension; hollowing their back under the rider's weigh causing a decrease in balance; a stiff jaw and neck due to a lack of acceptance of the bit and so on. For the horse trainer, these are problems to conquer in order to bring along a horse's training; for a horseback riding instructor, these problem behaviors tell us about our student's riding. When Trigger gets squeamish and strong, is Susie clamping her lower leg? When Brandy hollows his back, is John sitting down too hard? When Squirt locks his jaw and gets hard to steer is Linda locking her arms? Perhaps the bigger challenge instructors face is determining if these behaviors are horse training problems or *in response* to the rider. Determining this can take time and most often is some combination of horse and rider. On the other hand, examples of *desirable* body language include: the horse who relaxes its back clear through the tail, evidenced in a soft wing of the tail in rhythm the gait; a horse who drops its head and moves freely forward is no longer "fleeing" - this horse moves straighter and has a rider assisting in this accomplishment. Getting to know each horse's body language enables instructors and students to communicate more effectively with that individual horse.

RIDERS LEARNING FROM SCHOOLED HORSES. While this relationship is optimal for novice riders; riders at *all* levels benefit from riding a school master. Through consistency and quality of work, school masters *show* students what properly executed movements *feel* like. They give easily to their riders because they understand the work and exercises. Typically, seasoned school horses help to develop confidence and polished riding skills. These equine teachers provide support during lessons that greener horses cannot. School masters sense when a rider is over faced and respond to this with a helping hand. They are also able to "tell" on a rider who does something wrong - *in a nice way*. Most school masters have a certain "niche" of what they teach easily; therefore, meshing with certain programs and particular riders best. While some riding schools are lucky enough to groom "school masters"; those less fortunate, should encourage switching horses during lessons and short term leases to enable their students to benefit from a school master when the timing is right.

RIDERS LEARNING FROM GREEN HORSES. While a school master is a shepherd and a task master; a green horse provides a new world of discovery for a rider. Care needs to be taken to avoid over-mounting a very green rider on a very green horse; however, intermediate and advanced riders arrive at their skill level *by* riding greener horses as well as schooled mounts. Green horses teach riders to be more consistent and dependable. A rider's stability of seat, aids and a reasonable progression of lessons for a greener mount is required if progress is to be made. Furthermore, greener horses exhibit far more glee when they learn a new skill or accomplish something difficult. This becomes infectious. Riders who experience the satisfaction of having been a part of this learning process are generally highly motivated. Greener horses also tend to be a mirror. They reflect back to the rider, in a cause and effect fashion, feedback on uneven aids, unbalanced weight distribution and so on. While they might not be able to compensate for a rider, they benefit riders in revealing the need for better aids or balance. And last, green horses bring much more pure equus language into the equation; love and learning with these equines leads to "horse whisperers" in the making!

TIPS FOR FINDING SCHOOL HORSES:

In my *Tips for Teaching Safety in Your Riding Lessons*, I emphasize the importance *the horse* plays in helping to keep riding lessons as safe as possible. Horses are, in my opinion, our co-teaching partners. Therefore, what school horses you choose to accompany you in your teachings will have a profound effect on the success of your lessons. To parallel humans coming "of age" at 18 or 21 years; horses also come "of age" around 5 to 7 years of age. While instructors do teach riders on horses of younger ages, these horses are generally "in training" for being ridden and are obtaining schooling for that particular riding discipline. For the purpose of this topic, these tips cover the *search* for horses more schooled than the riders you will be teaching. For the selection of school horses, primary concerns are: appropriate level of training, size - age - temperament, price and availability. These concerns *are not* prioritized. You must do this by identifying your individual needs and preferences. Assuming that task is accomplished, lets look at ideas on how to *f i n d* these horses.

YOUR BEST RESOURCE IS A FRIEND YOU CAN TRUST. While an obvious statement .... put this statement into several contexts:

Your best resource is a friend you can trust buying or obtaining your next school horse from. While guarantees readily come with material items, it is as harder to "guarantee" a horse - much the same as it is hard to guarantee ourselves....meanwhile we do our best. Love might be blind, but trust is generally earned or lost. In working with this friend you can trust, you need to give consideration to: Can this friend supply sufficient reliable information about the horse? Is there a "return" option should things not work out? Will you be able to obtain the previous health information on the horse? Should this friend have *the ideal* school horse, but you do not *need* the horse until spring, can you "carry" this horse over the winter to get you both *to* spring? Will you be able to re-sell or provide a permanent home to the horse when your needs are met or it is time for retirement? *Meanwhile,* friends are gained by cultivating contacts you trust to buy your school horses *f r o m*!

Your best resource is a friend you can trust who knows of appropriate school horses for lease or loan. Many riding schools operate on the basis of lease agreements with owners/agents. Among the reasons for lease agreements are: an owner who can only be a seasonal horseback rider; an owner who rides once a week at best; a family horse that has been outgrown by the rider yet the family prefers to lease rather than sell the horse; etc. Other instructors in your area, local riding club leaders, blacksmiths, veterinarians (large and small), owners/managers of tack stores and sometimes feed stores *ALL* have the potential to convey information on prospective school horses for lease.

Your best resource is a friend you can trust who has seen "the perfect" school horse you must go see. While the previous scenarios indicate professionals in business - this scenario often includes your clients and other knowledgeable horsemen. Since going door to door in search of a suitable school horse is labor some, having a friend you can trust recommend a horse to consider is time saving. Give consideration to: Does *your* definition of the *perfect* school horse fit theirs? Have they seen this horse work in an environment similar to your school program? Will this horse be able to adapt to your stabling environment? Etc.

Your best resource is a friend you can trust which might be straight from the horse's mouth. Another words, like horses frequently choose their owners, some horses choose to *BE* school horses. Part of that choice is reflected in doing a good job as a school horse and moving from time to time to various programs through being sold. At times, horses not suited to their current job, get a chance to be a school horse. Other times, horses no longer able to work rigorously *(athletically)*, but are not ready for retirement either - shift to being a school horse enabling them to pull their weight, in a different way.

While I have outlined *your best resource* to be a number of different individuals - including the horse - once you get your school horse home, be sure to provide a well rounded loving environment and look forward to many enjoyable hours in the ring, field or trial.

TIPS FOR MAKING YOUR OWN SCHOOL HORSES:

Aside from the lifestyles of feral horses and horses who are pets, general *job* descriptions for horses include: competition horses, pleasure horses, racing horses, school horses, sport horses and work horses. While horses frequently wear different hats at different times in their lives, some horses easily alternate their hat from season to season, some from day to day and upon occasion from hour to hour! In making school horses, consider carefully, that some horses are more suited to the job of *teaching riding* than others.

School horses who are good at their job *ARE* able to discriminate when the rider has been over faced or when a rider needs a bit more of a challenge. While disposition, age, breed, health and previous training (if any) will guide your initial selection of a suitable horse to start making into a school horse, the entitlement of "school master" is *earned* through years of practice. Additionally, being a school horse or a school master at a particular level for a particular discipline does not guarantee a transfer to a different riding level or a different discipline. Thus, like our teaching skills, school horses provide dependable service for the level and discipline for which they are skilled.

EXPOSURE TO THE LESSON ENVIRONMENT AND THE OPPORTUNITY FOR OBSERVATION HELPS TO MOLD A SCHOOL HORSE. Naturally, if you will be using this school horse who is "in the making" to teach riders learning to canter, the horse in question should be able canter easily *and* provide the quality of canter stride that enables a novice rider the opportunity to sit comfortably and safely during their first experiences. These are skills a suitable school horse must be able to provide. But aside from the required skills a school horse in the making needs to learn, the opportunity to observe role models (other equines) with respect to *applying* these skills in an *actual* environment is invaluable. Horses are herd animals and they learn a tremendous amount from each other. Whenever and however possible, setting up mentorships with positive equine role models will move along your school horse's training. Frequently this can be done by inviting a more advanced rider mounted on your "school horse in the making" to join *a lesson* for which this horse is being trained. Your rider does not have to be a professional trainer. In fact, drawing upon your more advanced students (if available) is most satisfactory. Lets continue our example: the first canter experiences for novice riders. Ask the advanced rider to *role play* a novice rider for the canters during this class - this is helpful to the horse. Yet another way to enable school horses "in training" to gain mentorship from equine role models is to situate this horse in a stall or field with the opportunity to observe their role models in action. And last, it can be helpful to ride this horse yourself during the course of a lesson; however, be sure safety and your attention will not be compromised by the horse you are mounted on - this is not a time to train a youngster who demands attention.

BRINGING ALONG GREEN SCHOOL HORSES WITH YOUR MORE ADVANCED RIDERS IS A FUNDAMENTAL PROCESS. Only if you operate a very small riding school, will you be able to do *all* the riding yourself. Furthermore, many benefits result *for* more advanced students who have the opportunity to help you in preparing school horses. With respect to riding skills, more advanced students also provide an additional downward stepping stone for the school horses "to be." At times, it can be hard to emulate effectively, lesser riding skills, thus drawing upon your students ready for the opportunity to help with training a school horse under supervision is helpful to the horses and your program.

AND LAST, VERY FEW WELL PREPARED SCHOOL HORSES ACTUALLY GO "SOUR." All too frequently this description is used in reference to a school horse who has been over faced and is showing signs of confusion, frustration, or fatigue. School horses properly prepared, *enjoy* their job. Occasionally, a seasoned but bored or hurting school horse will make "sour" gestures. Health care should be investigated; changing careers considered and a lengthy vacation provided should that be determined a best first step to resolve a school horse "gone sour."

TIPS FOR GREEN RIDER/HORSE COMBO'S:

Most references on teaching horseback riding regard green horses combined with green riders with skepticism if not total discouragement. While this conservative posture is understandable, there *are* benefits for green horses and green riders learning together. Bear in mind, the principle reason riding instructors discourage green riders being paired with green horses is safety, unknown potential suitability and the heavy time requirements for supervision of these combinations. The secondary reason for discouraging this pairing is riding green horses produce sharper peaks and valleys in the learning curve. For green riders, green horses can be very discouraging or downright frustrating; meanwhile the green horse develops undesirable habits, at times irreversible. Understanding that instructors need to be on the lookout for these undesirable "valleys", here are a few examples of the majestical "peaks", of green riders learning with green horses.

QUICKLY, A SPECIAL FRIENDSHIP IS CULTIVATED WHEN GREEN RIDERS ARE LEARNING WITH GREEN HORSES WHICH PROVIDES FOR UNEQUALED PRIDE OF PERSONAL ACCOMPLISHMENT. Compatible green horse and rider combinations experience sheer joy while learning new skills together. *This* joy creates motivation. For these hand and glove combinations, riding instructors have little work to do to keep *either* horse or rider motivated. Whereas green riders, mounted on school horses or even school masters, can loose motivation because of the need for camaraderie rather than the parenting guidance of a schooled horse. Thus, to some instructors' dismay, certain green riders and green horses progress despite the predictions of the instructor onlooker!

GREEN HORSES ALSO SEND A STRONGER MESSAGE OF SUCCESS OR FAILURE REGARDING THE PROPER USE OF AIDS TO GREEN RIDERS. While school horses, by job description, need to be capable of *teaching* - putting out that helping hand (or hoof) so to speak; a green horse is not capable of teaching in this same fashion. Green horses simply react to their environment. So while a green horse cannot help in "leading the way", just by virtue of their lack of response or lack of understanding, this green horse is guiding the student. Since proper riding and training skills ARE based on the natural aids, improper aids or the improper sequence of aids simply do not work. Like a crisply focused picture, green horses provide cut and dry responses as they are learning. Once green horses have learned a new skill, less exact approximations of the aids will work; similar to a school horse. So in a way, green horses demand better riding skills, if the green horse and rider are to progress. For the green rider, the results are skills learned *thoroughly*, but often learned *slower* than when mounted on a school horse. After all, it does take time and practice to hone these better skills. Compatible green horses will be able to survive these "trial and error" periods, where incompatible green horses go progressively downhill with little relief. It is the job of an instructor, no matter how hard, to discourage incompatible combinations.

COMPATIBLE TEMPERAMENT IS THE STRONGEST RULE OF THUMB FOR SUCCESSFUL GREEN HORSE GREEN RIDER COMBINATIONS. The result of a green rider who scares a green horse is a high level of tension; a green horse who scares a green rider results in a rider who wants to quit riding. While a variety of "green" combinations *can* work, it is best to seek or encourage calm, not dull, tempered green horses for green riders. While this does not exclude hot *or* cold blooded horses, the warmer blooded horses do tend to fit this bill more naturally. Following temperament - size, age, breeding and athletic potential should also be considered. A more comfortable size eases the learning challenges for both horse and rider; horses *of* riding age should be sought (not too young or too old); breeding background *includes* how this horse was *raised* - those raised where riding was a daily part of the home lifestyle, generally results in a horse more eager to be ridden; and seeking horses who do not have to struggle, *athletically*, to carry the rider works out best. The rest will be up to your green rider and green horse .....to bond...... if this is in the stars. Do not be discouraged if it takes several attempts to find an appropriate green horse that the green r i d e r finds "compatible."

Chapter Three

CURRICULUM & LESSON ORGANIZATION

TIPS FOR LESSON PLANNING:

I ndividual lesson plans should be the result of a general curriculum structure. While a novice instructor should write out a written lesson plan in advance or follow a plan provided, a tenured instructor will be able to conduct a quality lesson with only a few mental notes in advance. Instructors who are "in training" should receive regular council on their lesson plans while experienced instructors should continually search for creative and different ways to teach the curriculum they are imparting. Regardless of the experience of the instructor, good lesson planning will include: *1) Advance preparations and student prerequisites needed to conduct the lesson 2) identification of the material to be covered 3) what the desired learning outcomes are 4) the teaching methods to be used 5) what methods will be used to determine the degree of student learning.*

EFFECTIVE LESSON PLANNING WILL ACTIVELY INVOLVE YOUR STUDENT. To regularly determine your students' goals, time constraints, financial abilities, health abilities and so on, enables you to do positive lesson planning. Most lesson programs and individuals are thorough about this when first signing a student up. However, be sure to source this information periodically from your regular students as well. Not only do student conditions change from time to time, but serious breakdowns in communication occur when students or instructors make assumptions in these areas. Effective lesson planning means respecting the importance of staying current with your student's goals and abilities. If your student volunteers this information rather regularly - great! But if not, tactfully go after it. Another important way to involve your student in lesson planning, is to invite them to contribute to your lesson plans. For example: a few simple questions like, "Charlotte, where do you feel the weakest? Let's work on that for the second half of the lesson" or "Randy, can you create an exercise of canter figures for the whole class to try during the next lesson?" *actively* involves your student. Active learning is d o i n g. Passive learning is receiving. Teacher requests that ask a student to: use what they have learned, create, or provide an example of *their* choice, results in active learning. The student is in charge of the "doing" not the teacher. Exercises you choose that focus on active learning (doing) will help students with motivation, allow for student creativity and help you determine how much your student has learned. Passive learning (receiving) is needed for increasing a student's awareness, knowledge and improving listening skills. Riding instructors tend to be heavy on passive learning lesson plans. Be sure you include active learning elements to your lessons - they are equally important for our students and us.

LESSONS PLANS SHOULD BE FLEXIBLE. Planning that includes a choice of exercises over a single approach produces much more flexibility once you get to the riding arena. Furthermore, for novice instructors, nothing is worse than not having planned enough! Since lesson plans should include: *1) Advance preparations and student prerequisites needed to conduct the lesson 2) identification of the material to be covered 3) what the desired learning outcomes are 4) the teaching methods to be used 5) what methods will be used to determine the degree of student learning.* There is a lot of room for the lesson to alter once we get to the ring. A well known example is: we have gotten to the ring, planned a lesson for work on flying lead changes with a new student who claims they are ready for this next skill, only to discover this rider has an interfering seat at the canter, little balance accomplished and the horse breaks gait a lot. Naturally, out goes the introductory lesson plan on flying changes and in goes the tactful lesson on basics. Another scenario in staying flexible with lesson planning would be adjusting your lunge lesson designed to work on improving your student's sitting trot when the neighbor's horses start running. Unfortunately your best lunge horse is also the one who always wants to go running with the neighbors and expresses this in brilliant passage which is a bit beyond the student's reach. Time to move to the indoor or switch the lesson plans that day!

TIPS FOR ESTABLISHING RIDING SKILL PREREQUISITES:

Those skills needed as a foundation for more advanced skills are *skill prerequisites*. In horseback riding instruction, your riding skill prerequisites should reflect both safety standards and quality standards. In many cases it will be helpful to share these riding skill prerequisites with your students and parents if you are teaching children. Riding skill prerequisites are an important part of curriculum planning. Our students come for riding instruction in order to avoid the trial and error learning system available to anyone learning how to ride on their own. Riding skill prerequisites are a major portion of the *wisdom* students seek from horseback riding instructors. These prerequisites are your *system* of riding instruction.

SKILL PREREQUISITES FOR ALL RIDING SKILLS, ARE A COMBINATION OF LESSER SKILLS MASTERED, PROPER KNOWLEDGE, CORRECT ATTITUDE AND PROPER FITNESS. The old adage - you never forget how to ride a bike is true only in some contexts. While it is obvious that preparing a student to attempt a *new* more difficult skill, requires steps *a*, *b* and *c* accomplished before going onto *d*; preparing a student to perform a skill they have done in the past, requires either "tuning" or at least "checking" their prerequisite skills before proceeding. Here is a typical scenario: Steve rode when he was young. In fact he was quite an accomplished rider. Now, 15 years later he is getting back into horseback riding and wants to fox hunt. He has never fox hunted; he showed hunters and jumpers as a youth. Naturally, Steve will need to get his riding muscles fit. He is quite confident on horseback with a proper attitude for the sport he plans to embark on. However, he knows *nothing* about hunting etiquette and protocol. So, to prepare Steve for fox hunting, aside from building his physical fitness and tuning his jumping timing, he principally will need to gain the necessary "fox hunting" knowledge to allow him to join the field and enjoy the experience.

SHARING SKILL PREREQUISITES WITH YOUR STUDENTS HELPS BOLSTER STUDENT MOTIVATION AND ENABLES YOUR STUDENTS TO CHART THEIR PROGRESS TOO. "Susie, in order for you to start over fences, you need to strengthen your lower leg position so you can hold the 2-point position in trot easily for 5 minutes straight. Then you will be fit enough in the proper jumping position to start jumping." It is best if you can develop your skill prerequisites in measurable terms for the student. For Susie, 5 minutes of 2-point performed *easily* is a clear measure. A few more examples are: "George, you need to be able to establish a balanced counter canter with soft, obedient simple changes of lead through the walk before Miss Dixie should be introduced to flying changes. Heather, before riding without stirrups, which is a great exercise for balance and strength, you should be able to drop and pick up either stirrup, one at a time during the walk and trot."

CHECKING SKILL PREREQUISITES CAN BE DONE THROUGH INFORMAL "TESTS" IN YOUR LESSONS. For skills, develop an exercise. For knowledge and attitudes, ask questions or request that your student write a paper. For fitness, assess respiration and sometimes even ask your students to take their pulse. When assessing skill prerequisite mastery, use speed, quality, accuracy and independence as criteria. Once your student is ready to proceed to the more advanced skill, their transition will be a smooth progression made safely with confidence.

TIPS FOR STEP BY STEP INSTRUCTION:

"Traditional" teaching is almost synonymous with step by step instruction. Building blocks; careful sequencing; step one must be satisfactorily completed before preceding onto step two are features of this method of instruction. Step by step instruction is logical. Step by step instruction is principally teacher paced. Researchers of various sports education agree, step by step instruction is preferred for beginners. The reason - ease of learning and safety. Beyond beginners, the effectiveness of step by step instruction compared to unstructured methods is a toss up. Researchers also agree the choice of which method to use beyond beginners, lies principally with student needs, timing and preferences. Additionally, some learners and some teachers *feel* more comfortable with step by step instruction. Thus these individuals seek and continue with traditional teaching practices throughout all levels of learning. While others, branch out to less structured methods. Most tenured instructors apply a combination of step by step methods *and* unstructured methods, allowing the student's needs and learning to guide the choice of when to be more structured and when to be less structured.

CREATING YOUR STEPS FOR STEP BY STEP INSTRUCTION, SHOULD BE BASED ON ACADEMIC STUDY OF THE AVAILABLE EQUESTRIAN LITERATURE AND YOUR PERSONAL PAST EXPERIENCES BOTH IN TEACHING AND RIDING. While many fine references and curriculum guides are emerging for horseback riding instructors, nonetheless, each lesson plan you develop should be a *creation* of your own. Step by step instruction is not a method of following a "recipe." Each instructor needs to embrace responsibility for the steps they use and plan for how they will navigate any potential problems that might arise due to their choice of steps. Step by step instruction is a method of instructor paced sequencing. This sequencing is principally founded on the principle that learning certain skills *first*, provides a foundation for increased success of learning other skills. Most clearly, this applies to the learning of less difficult skills prior to more difficult skills. Obvious examples of sequencing would be: learning how to jump a one foot fence before trying a four foot fence; learning how to guide a cooperative horse before attempting to guide a less cooperative horse; learning how to drive a single harnessed horse before driving a four in hand and so on. For learning more advanced skills and advanced skills of similar degrees of difficulty, step by step instruction still exists; however, the *sequencing* of steps from instructor to instructor will vary more greatly. For example, Susie is an intermediate rider. She wants to try her hand at both barrel racing and reining. Her instructor chooses to introduce her to reining first and barrel racing second. Their reasoning is: once she has ridden spins, stops and flying changes at slower speeds, she will be better prepared for riding the components of the barrel race. Meanwhile, another instructor who has a different student with the same desire chooses to introduce their rider to barrel racing first. This choice has been made because the rider's horse has barrel raced in the past and the reining maneuvers will be new to both horse and rider. This instructor feels the skills gained by the rider from learning the barrel racing first will help the rider in teaching the new skills of reining *to* their horse.

Ultimately, *managing your steps* **of step by step instruction, is just as important as the initial choice of steps.** This is a combination of being a doctor, lawyer and Indian chief all in one. Be prepared to problem-solve problem areas; be prepared to defend your choice of steps and be prepared to require compliance until some degree of success has had a chance to occur. Managing your steps of instruction in these areas will be central to the success of utilizing step by step instruction effectively. Managing your steps of instruction will also mean remaining flexible and ready to streamline your steps of instruction for improved results. While you have determined certain steps work best in a high number of instances, each learning environment remains *individual*. Assuming the steps you have grown to trust will *always* work is somewhat unrealistic. Remaining flexible in managing your steps while adjusting some steps as needed will achieve the basic principle of: learning certain skills/knowledge first, *eases* the learning of other skills/knowledge.

TIPS FOR LESS STRUCTURED INSTRUCTION:

"Less structured" or "unstructured" instruction, simply means the instructor is sacrificing a *teacher* paced lesson plan. While an instructor who applies a "less structured" lesson, does not present a traditional lesson plan of step by step instruction, their lesson/s will still reflect important principles of curriculum progression. Often, the *result* of less structured lessons, will be "steps" of instruction. It is rather like being *told* the correct answer or being encouraged to *explore* and *search* for the correct answer. In step by step instruction, the instructor determines and shares the steps to be taken. In less structured instruction, the student is presented with an environment suitable to explore and search. Both forms of instruction provide similar feedback to the student regarding success and failure.

REASONS FOR PROVIDING "LESS STRUCTURED" LESSONS INCLUDE: ENCOURAGING STUDENT INDEPENDENCE, THE NEED FOR VARIETY, WAYS TO INCREASE STUDENT MOTIVATION, MEANS TO REDUCE BOREDOM AND SO ON. Additionally, this approach to instruction results in more student initiated activities and thus more student engagement. The student helps to steer their instruction by making choices, solving problems, generating new ideas to try, running experiments, and so on. Examples of less structured lessons are:

- Leaving the topic/s to discuss in a lecture class up to student requests, i.e. *starting* with questions and answers
- Asking a particular student to prepare a contest to play during the next lesson and asking them to keep their contest planned, *private* until shared at the next lesson

- Assigning each member of a group riding lesson to be an instructor's assistant one time, during the upcoming semester of riding. When it is the rider's turn to be the "assistant" they share in developing the lesson plan for that upcoming day and attend that lesson *unmounted* to be an assistant to the instructor for the day
- By interrupting a step by step lesson that seems to be going stale, then asking the student/s to re-direct the lesson in an area of their choice
- Using a suggestion box at your barn to solicit ideas for less structured lessons

TIME FRAMES FOR LESS STRUCTURED LESSONS BECOME QUITE VARIABLE; SOMETIMES HELPFUL, SOMETIMES COUNTERPRODUCTIVE. While individual student learning rates contribute to this dimension, less structured lessons, in part, depend on the student's contributions. Many of the student needed contributions are linked less to individual learning rates (which are measurable) and more to the artistic and cooperative side of student contributions. Therefore be prepared to be more flexible with your time management areas.

LESS STRUCTURED INSTRUCTION REQUIRES AN INSTRUCTOR TO BE VERY WELL ORGANIZED AND PREPARED FOR A GREATER NUMBER OF UNFORESEEN POSSIBILITIES. Due to this factor, more tenured horseback riding instructors tend to be more comfortable with this approach to instruction. Furthermore, since the bulk of instruction for horseback riding occurs in groups, instructors new to teaching horseback riding manage to maintain better class control with step by step instruction; at least initially.

MEETING STUDENT PERFORMANCE OBJECTIVES OF A CURRICULUM CAN BE HARDER TO PREDICT WHEN USING SOLELY THE "LESS STRUCTURED" LESSON APPROACH. Since instructors are continually developing their sixth sense of how much progress will be achieved by students due to given exercises (student performance objectives), an instructor who widely uses the less structured lesson approach can have difficulty evaluating student learning. Setting student performance objectives helps to keep us on track and our students on track.

FOR INSTRUCTORS, SHIFTING TO LESS STRUCTURED LESSONS CAN BE A BREATH OF FRESH AIR. Instructors who have been performing volume step by step instruction, particularly at one level of instruction are subject to becoming burned-out or bored. Using either a combination of step by step instruction together with less structured lessons or shifting, for a period of time, to less structured lessons will ease these forces. Keeping us energized has value for all!

TIPS FOR TEACHING PRIVATE LESSONS:

Typically, for horseback riding instruction, private lessons are most commonly used for very novice or very advanced riders. These two levels of riders greatly benefit from the individual attention provided by private lessons. While riders between these two extremes occasionally insist on taking *only* private lessons, *all riders* will benefit from a mixture of private, semi-private and group lessons.

UNIQUELY, PRIVATE LESSONS ALLOW FOR TAILORING THE LESSON TO AN INDIVIDUAL'S NEEDS. Some rider issues and problems are best addressed in private lessons. For example: Susie has been having a hard time getting her large pony to pick up the left lead canter. Her aids have been reasonably correct, but the pony still picks up the incorrect lead. You advise Susie to take a private lesson next week to focus on resolving this problem. This private lesson will enable you to carefully evaluate *her* situation. You will have adequate time for Susie to try various exercises in search of a workable solution for getting this pony's left lead. Plus, if you need to lunge the pony or ride the pony a little, these activities will not take away from other students' time.

STUDENTS WHO NEED TO BE "TALKED THROUGH THE SKILL" WILL BENEFIT FROM TAKING A PRIVATE LESSON. The step by step process of talking a student through a skill is called *prompting*. These are commands; commands with little or no theory. The result feels like the rider is a puppet on a string. The instructor is, in a sense, riding the horse through the student. Particularly for areas such as *improving timing* or *improving the quality* of existing riding skills, this teaching technique is hard to beat. Prompting produces better aids and balance of the rider which in turn produces more correct sensations and performance from the horse. While it is possible to apply *prompting* techniques in lessons of any size, prompting in private lessons has a higher chance of producing a more correct riding *habit* - simply because of the additional time in one stretch. Since this technique requires the complete attention of the instructor, for semi-private and group lessons, it should only be used for short portions of those lessons. *Prompting* unquestionably develops *quality* performance skills; however, instructors who rely heavily on this technique are in danger of developing instructor dependent students. During the course of a riding program, prompting techniques should always be balanced with theoretical information, delayed feedback and other teaching techniques in order to cultivate independence in horseback riding. Prompting should be used as a tool to teach with, not the *only* tool of teaching horseback riding.

PRIVATE LESSONS ENCOURAGE STUDENTS TO FOCUS. Distractions by other students in a lesson can interfere with learning. While the social elements of a semi-private and group lesson are desirable to many students, this very feature can divide attention and reduce student focus. While it is the instructor's job to keep reasonable control of such distractions, realistically, shifting certain students to a private lesson is a possible solution. While this does not have to be a permanent arrangement, students who experience a lesson environment which *assists* them to focus, soon become more focused regardless of the environment. The benefits of increased learning due to increased focus are *very* motivational.

PRIVATE LESSONS ALSO HELP TO BUILD POSITIVE STUDENT - INSTRUCTOR RAPPORT. Though a well taught lesson of any size will promote a positive rapport with students, private lessons have one feature cornered: *privacy between students and instructors.* It is due to this private element, that *one on one* lessons leap ahead when in comes to *building* positive student rapport. Any problems of unhealthy competition with other students is eliminated. Undivided attention is provided *to* the student from the instructor. Private lessons are more intimate. Trust and free flowing inquiry from students to instructors develops quickly. As you get to know your student better, a more positive rapport is easier to achieve. Private lessons provide *more time* for this to happen.

TIPS FOR SEMI-PRIVATE LESSONS:

A semi-private lesson consists of two riders. The most characteristic element of the semi-private lesson is "who are the two students?" Sometimes "who rides together" is an arrangement of convenience for students. Sisters or friends ride together because of car pooling needs; husbands and wives upon occasion, insist on riding together - since this *is* an activity they "share." *These are conditions we inherit.* Working with inherited conditions while continuing to provide meaningful, safe lessons is simply a part of our job. Yet for other semi-private lessons, "who are the two students?" becomes *our* choosing. This flexibility allows for considerable teaching creativity. Lets look at ideas for pairing students of a semi-private lesson; both common place and creatively contrived.

MOST COMMON IS TO PAIR RIDERS BASED ON SIMILAR SKILLS, EXPERIENCE AND AGE. Therefore, most points during these lessons will readily apply to *both* students. For instructors, the lesson planning is simplified and for the students, the terms used, general language, lesson topics and instructional feedback will all blend smoothly. Additionally, advantageous group lesson dynamics of *visual examples, peer review and team spirit* are also easily achieved for semi-private lessons when the two students are quite similar. But in spite of these very positive elements, there does exist a down side to this pairing: *overt* competition developing between the two students of a semi-private lesson. *Healthy* competition stretches a fine line; be on the look out for excessive discouragement, lack of appreciation or inflated goals voiced between the two students. These are some warning signs that "team spirit" has been lost to "overt competition." Good resolutions to this dilemma are as varied as the individuals whom fall prey; however, an instructor must thoughtfully and tactfully address this problem *whether or not* these students remain classmates.

TRY PAIRING A MORE ADVANCED RIDER WITH A LESS ADVANCED RIDER OF THE SAME BODY TYPE. Now, the similar aspect of the semi-private lesson is the riders' body conformation and how these riders *use* their body (or need to). For example, long legged riders initially have difficulty *controlling* the length of their leg. While long legs for riding are generally considered an advantage, *initially* it rarely feels that way to the novice rider struggling to control noodle "ish" long legs. Lets, move to the riding ring: you have arranged for this struggling noodle "ish" long legged rider to share several lessons with a more advanced rider whom recently conquered this problem. During these lessons, you emphasize the steps from which the more advanced rider benefited. Additionally, you encourage dialogue *between* these two students about this problem. Their descriptions and questions between each other will be *different, yet just as meaningful* as the instructor-student dialogue. A student who just conquered a problem such as noodle "ish" long legs, clearly recalls, with appreciation and enthusiasm, the elements which lead them to transforming this problem. They *are* a living testimonial!

CONSIDERABLE BENEFIT IS ALSO GAINED BY PAIRING THE TRAINING PROBLEMS OF HORSES IN A SIMILAR "BIG BROTHER, LITTLE BROTHER" FASHION. Whether our lessons are with our string of school horses, or riders with their own mounts, or a mix, *pairing* horses for "mentorship" has positive merit. While the "observational" learning of horses has yet to gain much scientific focus, ask any seasoned instructor or trainer of the abilities of horses to learn from each other. Some examples of helpful pairing would be: choosing a dependable, willing horse to help coax a reluctant greener horse through a stream crossing; selecting a horse with correct lengthening in the trot to share a lesson with a horse who only speeds up; pairing a horse who *will* canter home from the last barrel with a horse who always rushes the last barrel, knocks it over then flies home. Because the training of horses is part of a riding instructor's concern, utilizing meaningful pairings of *horses,* plus the pairings of *riders* is just basic.

Meanwhile there are many more types of semi-private lessons that are creative and successful. Give your ideas a try. You can always "re-group" if a particular pairing does not work well. Have fun!

TIPS FOR TEACHING GROUP LESSONS:

Lesson size has a direct bearing on an instructor's approach to giving a lesson. Group lessons typically range in numbers from a small group of three or four to larger groups of six or more. *Very* large groups of more than ten are less common and generally have more disadvantages than advantages except for "clinic" environments. Meanwhile compared to semi-private or private lessons, group lessons provide *special* and *invaluable* opportunities for instructors and students alike. *All* students should ride some of the time in group lessons; lets look at why:

GROUP LESSONS PROVIDE MANY MORE VISUAL EXAMPLES FOR STUDENTS AND INSTRUCTORS TO DRAW UPON. In private lessons and even in semi-private lessons, the riding instructor is most often the demonstrator. While this is normal and desirable for providing those "good example" demonstrations, this approach can be limiting for visually evaluating *problem* areas. Certainly instructors can try to provide a "bad example", but rarely are these efforts very exact. Assuming instructors are teaching riders well beneath their own skill level, when an instructor manufactures an unstable lower leg position to "demonstrate", different *overall* ramifications result than what happens with riders who *have* an unstable lower leg position. Therefore, it is most helpful for instructors to compare similar problems in students and for students to watch each other in addition to instructor demonstrations. Furthermore, watching other riders of a group lesson provides the opportunity for students to witness and study the benefits of each newly achieved riding skill. Some of the unspoken visual messages they will get are: how this new skill affects the rider's balance; how this new skill affects the horse; how this new skill increases their effectiveness and so on.

UNIQUE TO GROUP LESSONS IS THE OPPORTUNITY FOR MEANINGFUL PEER REVIEW. Instructor guided peer review is a powerful teaching tool. Instructors who orchestrate peer review during group lessons promote higher levels of cognitive learning, provide time for observational learning and encourage *constructive* peer review. For example: While a particular group lesson is working on improving their transitions from trot to canter and canter to trot, the instructor isolates one or two riders of the group who are having more difficulty. Then, the instructor re-organizes the group so the riders having difficulty are practicing while the others are resting. The resting students are invited by the instructor to formulate solutions on how these particular students might improve their transitions. With guidance from the instructor, these students' solutions are then shared and put into motion by the riders practicing. Next, the students switch. The resting riders now resume their practicing. The instructor asks those riders who have been having more difficulty to observe and point out elements they see their peers achieving which seem to directly relate to better quality transitions; *valuable* student dialogue.

"TEAM SPIRIT" AND "FRIENDLY COMPETITION" RESULT FROM WELL ORGANIZED GROUP LESSONS. Instructor boosted morale, while important, is still *different* that peer boosted morale. At times, what students *NEED* is the boost of their peers. Peers support each other, in ways unavailable to instructors. Thus, group lessons are a wonderful way to provide opportunities for this. Allowing and encouraging occurrences of peer support will help bolster morale and achieve "team spirit" and "friendly competition" in your lessons.

GROUP LESSONS ALLOW FOR BOTH *GROUP ACTIVITIES* AND *ONE ON ONE INSTRUCTOR TIME.* Equally important in group lessons is individual attention, periodically, for each group member. For example, in novice level lessons, this is often achieved by one student trotting to the end of the file, or one student at a time doing a prescribed pattern. With advanced students, a further advantage is gained: while one student gets a few minutes of individual instruction, the remainder of the group can have independent time to practice. Independent riding time encourages students to *apply* skills and knowledge. The result is students learn to experiment and sort out problems as they arise, thus reducing instructor dependence!

Chapter Four

INSTRUCTIONAL PLANNING

TIPS FOR INTRODUCING NEW MATERIAL:

During 1986 I conducted an empirical survey research study on the teaching behaviors of expert horseback riding instructors when teaching a *new* riding skill. This study asked: from a list of proven teaching behaviors of general sports education, which behaviors do expert instructors prefer to use when teaching a new riding skill and how much do these instructors value the teaching behaviors listed? The teaching behaviors list was developed from empirical studies on effective teaching behaviors for sports such as basketball, football, tennis, golf, etc; no studies were found at that time on ERIC regarding the teaching behaviors of horseback riding instructors. In short, this study revealed expert riding instructors use a *wide* variety of teaching behaviors although the majority of these equestrian experts lack higher education degrees in teaching. Of the 79 respondents, almost half were male; most were between 31 and 50 years of age; 57% had 16 - 25 + years experience teaching *horseback riding* and 96% taught novice students at least *some* of the time. All disciplines of riding were represented. *SINCE* the introduction of "new material" for horseback riding is rooted in improving *riding skills*, lets look at what our experts reported they use and value for teaching a new riding skill to a student.

TEACHER TASK ANALYSIS: Our experts placed a heavy emphasis on the importance of instructors preparing for teaching a new riding skill by: 1) determining and considering student needs 2) planning for teaching the skill through either breaking the skill down into parts and then connecting them *or* teaching the whole skill and perfecting the skill through repetitions; however, they were equally divided on which approach they personally preferred for teaching a new skill.

PREPARING STUDENTS FOR LEARNING: Our experts were in agreement that preparing students for learning is *fundamental.* Introducing a skill, stating and checking prerequisites, identifying how a skill applies to riding, identifying student performance objectives and directing students' focus during demonstrations were all teaching behaviors they used frequently in teaching.

LECTURE, BLACKBOARDS, FILMS AND VIDEOS: While all of these teaching behaviors were *valued* by our experts, this group of instructors infrequently used these teaching behaviors for teaching a new motor skill in horseback riding instruction. They indicated this was mostly due to a lack of available equipment.

DEMONSTRATIONS: Our experts were almost unanimous in providing an initial demonstration of the skill before student practice. During this initial demonstration, these instructors reported they provide information on: 1) what to look for 2) what to look at 3) what to do 4) other skills that relate to this skill 5) how to check performance results 6) how to remediate common problems. However, these instructors also cautioned on the dilemma of "information overload. " Their solution to this problem was to deliver information gradually over time as students progress. Almost half of our experts identified they do not ask their *students* to talk the demonstrator through the skill prior to student practice; though take note: this teaching behavior and others which involve *student talk* of verbal cues and mediation *prior to practice* results in quicker learning and longer retention according to sports researchers. Again, our experts were almost unanimous in using the teaching behavior of performing a *second demonstration* after the students' initial practice to show chief faults of students' first practice. This behavior is *also* highly regarded by sports researchers. Meanwhile our experts frequently provide time for student questions before student practice but far less frequently provide time for students to describe the skill or mentally rehearse the skill prior to practice.

STUDENT PRACTICE: Ninety-nine percent of our experts use the following teaching behaviors 1) direct the student to concentrate on how the practice feels 2) identify performance qualities desired of initial student practice 3) identify performance qualities desired of future practice 4) observe practice and correct errors as they occur 5) talk the student through the skill 6) intersperse practice time with practice on other skills. Furthermore, over 75% of these experts correct errors as they occur 75-100% of the time and almost 60% direct their students to concentrate on how the practice feels 75-100% of the time. This does, however, raise a question since 49% of these experts also reported they rarely use the teaching behavior of: remaining silent during most of (initial) practice. Too much "teacher-talk" can interfere with student concentration and students' perception of their riding skills. Do horseback riding instructors tend to talk too much?

INSTRUCTOR FEEDBACK AND SKILL CONFIRMATION: All experts reported they use three behaviors to provide feedback when teaching a new riding skill and over 70% use these behaviors 75-100 % of the time: 1) provide feedback immediately 2) critique practice - desirable and undesirable parts 3) suggest how to improve next practice attempt. Conversely, our experts reported they do not tend to use the teaching behavior of delaying feedback to a student which is quite popular in other sports. With respect to skill confirmation, expert riding instructors seem to be divided on what method is best. Some feel only execution of skills counts; while others feel verbal questions are an important facet in determining skill mastery *together* with practice exercises. Certainly, since riding instructors often try to determine skill mastery at the end of a lesson when students may be tired, the latter method holds merit; adding further strength to the belief that learning and performance are not always synonymous.

TIPS TO VARY THE DEMONSTRATIONS WE PROVIDE:

In sports education, demonstrations are the single most teaching technique used to introduce a new skill. Demonstrations create a mental picture to follow - as simple as monkey see, monkey do. Once our students begin to try their hand at a new skill, demonstrations remain a vital method we use to provide feedback to the student about the quality of their practice. Naturally, it is very important to provide a quality demonstration, but instructor concerns that only a "flawless" demonstration will do, is an extreme attitude. Bare in mind, there are two facets to a demonstration: the physical demonstration the student watches and the verbal dialogue that accompanies the demonstration. Sports education research indicates that verbal dialogue for beginners should be kept to a minimum. Important components for an effective demonstration are: *direct your students' focus, repeat the demonstration several times and critique the demonstration*. While the instructor is and should be the primary demonstrator, lets look other ways to vary the demonstrations we provide.

ASKING ONE OF YOUR CAPABLE STUDENTS TO PROVIDE A DEMONSTRATION IS VERY MEANINGFUL. Try inviting a student from a more advanced class to demonstrate a particular riding skill being learned by another class. Organizing such a demonstration in advance, compliments your advanced rider's skills and provides a role model aside from the instructor for novice students to learn from. Carefully choosing your student role models and encouraging lesser skilled students to learn from them, builds team work and motivation. Surprisingly, student demonstrators will often be able to address the "pains of learning" easier than instructors. When your role model student provides the verbal dialogue along with their physical demonstration, *w e*, the instructors, get the chance to learn what that student demonstrator feels is most helpful for learning that particular skill. Choosing a class member to provide a demonstration for improving a particular skill, is also effective.

Take care not to develop a "class favorite" for demonstrating duties. Instead, periodically, give various students the chance to demonstrate those skills they are strong at. If the student can demonstrate desirable *and* undesirable examples of a particular riding skill, this will give you even more to work with. Learning and teamwork is developed in a group lesson by having the lesser skilled students talk a student demonstrator through the repeats of a demonstration. Happily this teaching technique also encourages your students to pay closer attention to demonstrations!

DON'T BE AFRAID TO SEIZE THE MOMENT WITH A WORTHY DEMONSTRATION. While we "plan" the majority of demonstrations provided to our students, there are wonderful spontaneous moments in lessons where a demonstration opportunity knocks on our door. Seize that moment! Some examples are: In a beginner lesson, suddenly Susie gets on a roll with her posting - it clicked! She is the first of the group to get the rhythm and keep it. Ask the remainder of the class to watch her progress while they rest. Then have Susie rest while they practice. As she observes their practice, she might have some additional helpful hints for her classmates. Meanwhile her classmates get the benefit of her additional demonstration of posting while she practices. In an intermediate lesson, a green but older horse discovers chewing the bit and proper flexing at the gullet. Wow! How different this horse's balance and top line become almost immediately. Although the overall lesson that day has been on proper use of the driving aids, flexion and self carriage has been worked on as a general theme for months. Seize the moment - interrupt the current lesson you are teaching and allow this student and horse to show off their quantum leap. In an advanced lessons where "improvements" tend to outweigh the "night and day - WOW" type progress, try encouraging your *students* to seize the moment and share a demonstration of their measurably improved skill as it occurs. Seizing the moment with a demonstration is downright refreshing for students and instructors - it is a measure of accomplishment.

TIPS FOR WRAPPING UP A LESSON:

A verbal summary by the instructor is probably the most commonly used method to wrap up a lesson followed by fielding any questions students might have at the closure of a lesson. However, wrapping up a lesson is also a time where the instructor should also be determining how much the students have learned thus far. Riding skill mastery should be determined through verbal questions and practice exercises. Effective planning for future lessons depends on properly assessing learning. While the practice portion of our lessons will provide us some measure of learning, lets look at some ways to wrap up a lesson that will shed further light on just how much our students have learned.

WHILE INSTRUCTORS ALWAYS WANT TO END UP ON A "GOOD" NOTE IN A LESSON, THIS MAY NOT BE ENTIRELY POSSIBLE IF WE CHOOSE TO CLOSE WITH A FINAL EXERCISE. Wrapping up with a final exercise is a one shot deal - sort of an informal test. Be sure to prepare your students for the need to defer to the next lesson or their next ride for further practice, if their execution of this final exercise is less than perfect. Particularly if a final exercise is done one at a time for group lessons, this will allow you focus on the individual improvement each student has made. Furthermore, lengthy continuous practice if a student is not tiring, tends to provide better performance than shorter practice sessions unless that particular riding skill has been thoroughly learned. Therefore continuous practice during the concentrated part of your lesson can be misleading for assessing riding skills. Thus, some of the peak performance of practice you are seeing your students accomplish during the lesson, may not "hold" when you ask your students to do a final exercise one at a time. For example: Your students have been practicing making round, rather than egg shaped circles. Most of the lesson has been devoted to this in one fashion or another. As a wrap up final exercise, you ask your students to perform, one at a time, a simple pattern of two circles in each direction. Those students that experience a decrease in skill during this last exercise should not become alarmed - all they need is additional practice time to thoroughly accomplish getting their circles round on a regular basis.

ANOTHER WAY TO ASSESS STUDENT LEARNING AND WRAP UP YOUR LESSON, IS TO ASK EACH STUDENT TO REPEAT AN ACTIVITY OR EXERCISE OF THE LESSON THEY HAVE MOST OR LEAST ACCOMPLISHED, IN THEIR OPINION. Student perceptions of their learning at times do not match ours. Sometimes we see improvements coming down the pike, but they have yet to feel them. Likewise, sometimes our students will experience a significant breakthrough in a particular area during the course of a lesson which we have not recognized. Where "feel" is concerned, our students can experience a sensory "bingo" unknown to us. Where theory is concerned, our students can make a connection which enables them to better understand how their aids work.... also unknown to us. Therefore, encouraging our student's input with a final activity of the *student's choice* will help bring these matters to the light. When a student chooses to repeat an activity which they have *least* accomplished to date, we are able to provide a final critique on their weak points which helps to build the next lesson plan.

INSTRUCTORS CAN ALSO WRAP UP A LESSON WITH STUDENT QUESTIONING WHICH ASKS THE STUDENT TO APPLY WHAT THEY HAVE LEARNED. For example, a particular lesson has been on introducing the lateral bending of the horse. The instructor has prepared several questions to wrap up this lesson: "George, you have accomplished some lateral bending with Trigger today. What figures aside from the ones you have practiced, will become smoother and better balanced if Trigger is bending?" "Cheryl, equate lateral bending of the horse to some exercises humans do to limber up." Answers to questions such as these will help instructors determine their student's level of cognitive learning.

TIPS FOR ASSIGNING HOMEWORK:

All levels and types of students benefit from homework. Homework ties lessons together. Homework helps students progress *between* lessons. Homework provides students a sense of direction for what practice and study will best benefit them, *individually*. For sports skills, "homework" can be broken down into three general categories: 1) practice of exercises 2) improving a rider's fitness/flexibility 3) increasing or deepening a rider's understanding of theory.

When students accomplish homework between lessons, their foundation is strengthened. This valuable time spent, creates exploration which helps your students process and internalize the instruction they have received; better preparing them for their next lesson. What a teacher's reward it is to have a student come for their next lesson full of comments and questions because they practiced what they learned! Lets take a closer look at these categories of homework:

WHEN WE ASSIGN EXERCISES TO PRACTICE, WE ARE ESTABLISHING PERFORMANCE OBJECTIVES WE WOULD LIKE OUR STUDENT/S TO ACHIEVE. Performance objectives should include, under what *conditions* this practice should take place and to what *degree* the skill should be achieved. Examples of this would be: "Susie, your circles need to be rounder. During the middle of your rides, practice circles until you can get one *out of every three perfectly* round." "Randy, you need to be able to ride on a lighter contact. Several times before your next lesson, stay in the ring so Rocket will not get pumped up going across the country. In the ring, trust Rocket some and loosen up your grip *to the strength of a handshake*. If he gets strong and you are tempted to pull, do so only to make a <u>downward</u> transition. Wait to transition upward again, until you feel organized. Be alerted, you may be doing a lot of transitions downward.... at first!"

STRENGTHENING OR FLEXIBILITY HOMEWORK FOR 9 OUT OF 10 STUDENTS IS ROUTINELY USEFUL. Horseback riding requires strength but only at times. Riders need to build the *sometimes* needed strength yet stay flexible enough *not to use this strength* a good deal of the time. As students progress, this scale gets tipped one direction or the other. Timely homework creates those one out of ten riders.

FOR INCREASING AND DEEPENING A RIDER'S UNDERSTANDING OF THEORY - READING, DEBATES AND AUDITING RIDERS AT A HIGHER LEVEL ARE IDEAL HOMEWORK AREAS. When riders need to increase their knowledge, make good use of the abundance of books available on learning how to ride [better]. Naturally, *be sure* you have read the books you recommend and be prepared to respond to any confusion a student might encounter from reading a book. Even more abundant and more user friendly in length are suitable articles. A helpful angle for individualizing an article *to* a student, is to prepare the student's study of an article through identifying those portions to pay particular attention to. Furthermore, try taking *your* pen to paper to jot down some notes to this student on their article copy. This is an opportunity to tie particular points of the article to *their* riding. Should you disagree with any part of the article, jot this down too - *debate* helps to challenge your student's academic exploration of theory. Aside from literary forms of debate, student to student debates make nice homework assignments as well. Pairing two students up to research and debate a particular topic, returning with an agreed upon position is fun for students and new close friends can be made this way! Last, auditing riders at a higher level is like *moving pictures* in a book. Though auditing is not the study of written or spoken word, what a student observes, gathers and deducts is priceless to their knowledge and learning about horseback riding!

TIPS FOR INCORPORATING THEORY INTO YOUR LESSON:

Principles of riding equitation, horse training, equine and human physiology are just a few of the academic topics we teach about during horseback riding instruction. While our students come to us to learn how to ride a horse or how to better ride their own horse, riding instruction *should* encompass progressing the student's theoretical knowledge as well as cultivating their physical skills. For the student, riding and training theory takes study and application. For the instructor, teaching theory means progressing your student's understanding of useful and important principles. Some instructors are best at creating lesson plans that are a series of riding exercises. Other instructors are best at creating lesson plans that are a "classroom" lecture/discussion on horseback. *All* instructors should strive to be able to easily provide an exercise lesson, lecture/discussion lesson or a combination thereof. Lets look at some ways to incorporate "theory instruction" into your lessons.

COVERING THEORY IN YOUR RIDING LESSONS WILL TAKE UP RIDING TIME - THIS IS NORMAL. Lets say properly introducing a new *exercise* takes roughly 5 minutes. Now take this teacher talk a further step. Lets say introducing a new exercise that also requires new theory to be *understood*, and by the way, this is a 45 minute group lesson of 6 riders and naturally a number of the students are raising their hands with questions in a quest to understand the theory you are covering. Easily, 5 minutes can stretch into 15-20 minutes. For the ride, ride, ride, riders, nearly half of their lesson devoted to this more "in depth" theory may seem boring, inappropriate or even a downright waste of their money. One way to accomplish a block of time devoted to theorizing is to *begin* your lesson with a familiar exercise that will physically tire out your student/s. Then, finish your lesson with the lengthy theory portion that prepares them for their next lesson. Hopefully your students' normal resistance to "theorizing" will melt into increased appreciation! Certainly, the most traditional structure for teaching theory during a riding lesson follows this sequence: introduction (involving some theory), student practice (riding), more theory (during a rest period needed anyhow), more practice (applying theory under instruction or trial and error), and wrap up of the lesson (through discussion or exercises that determine students' understanding and/or their ability to apply the theory taught). This traditional lesson sequence means no big chunks of time are spent all at once on theorizing. Sounds good and probably most often this is the best approach, but riding theory *misunderstood* can lead to poor riding skills let alone safety problems or a lack of confidence in one's teacher. Another step away from the traditional sequence of incorporating theory into a riding lesson, is to respond to emergency times in a lesson by *STOPPING* your lesson to clear up a theory misunderstanding you have been observing and sensing. These "emergency" times might involve safety issues, but more often than not, they are those times when a student has a gross lack of skill performance, the student is crying or upset, or the student is frustrated or confused and they are taking it out on the horse. Better understanding of riding theory assists in developing proper riding skills and contributes to pressing through learning plateau's.

ALSO UTILIZE HOMEWORK ASSIGNMENTS TO PREPARE AND PROGRESS YOUR STUDENTS' THEORY. Helpful riding homework assignments include: read a certain article or book, go to a particular clinic or seminar to ride or audit, rent a specific video to study a useful portion, go on a field trip to watch a horse show or demonstration, work with another student to prepare an assignment, go with another student to a library to research a particular riding theory, etc. For the homework assignments you make, *be sure* to follow up on your students' progress. Charting your student's theory learning from your lessons due to homework and other sources, should be recognized (and rewarded) plus guided (if confusion develops). This is *all* a part of teaching.

TIPS FOR RECOMMENDING INDEPENDENT STUDY:

Broadly, *independent study* with respect to horseback riding instruction, refers to one of two circumstances. The first and most common is that study performed outside the instructional arena to benefit a student's horseback riding skills. Examples of this type of independent study are: homework, assignments or other initiatives by the student. The second is a sabbatical like extended period of study. Examples are: going to a horseback riding summer camp for three months; taking a working student position for the spring, summer or fall; going abroad to study and so on. The first type of independent study is a basic component of instruction and thus, a routine part of quality horsemanship programs. Conversely, a small portion of horseback riders participate in sabbatical like periods of independent study. Usually students who are young with summers available or those individuals preparing to work in the horse industry seek sabbatical type experiences. The results from a sabbatical period of study are usually monumental. Let us examine both of these types of independent study more closely.

TYPICALLY, HORSEBACK RIDING LESSONS ARE MOUNTED; THE PRACTICE OF SKILLS OCCUPIES THE MAJORITY OF "LESSON TIME." THUS, COGNITIVE LEARNING ABOUT HORSEBACK RIDING IS RELEGATED TO BRIEF ARENA LECTURES, AUDITING LESSONS AND A HEAVY RELIANCE ON *INDEPENDENT STUDY* OF RECOMMENDED RESOURCES. These recommended resources include: books, articles, videos and occasionally - audio tapes. Independent study at home or in a barn library cements a student's knowledge, understanding and their ability to apply solutions to problems on horseback. This study is the mental practice needed to master new concepts. Both adults *and* children need to know why they are practicing certain skills and how those individual riding skills fit into the whole. While instructors do *identify* these components during mounted lessons, all students need "cognitive study time." For this reason, some riding schools provide lecture lessons to compliment mounted lessons. This structure is very sound from an educational standpoint of view. But useful independent study has rules. Consider these rules the *instructor's checklist*:

Rule #1: Select and recommend references you have reviewed *cover to cover*.

Rule #2: Determine how much time your student has available to devote to independent study. This might affect your selection choices.

Rule #3: Choose references that will clarify and support the topics of your lessons. Avoid recommending more advanced material unless this is done to *prepare* the student for a forthcoming lesson.

Rule #4: Develop dependable methods to assess your student's independent study.

Methods include: a short essay of the reference; a question and answer session *you* lead to assess learning and/or to answer student questions; pose a debate between several students on the reference with respect to a particular part of the content; during a lesson, draw upon the student to identify the content of a reference that relates to the lesson at hand; etc.

While riding instructors are responsible for initiating *lesson related* independent study, quite frequently conscientious students will pursue further independent study themselves. Along with the above check list, periodically ask your students if they have pursued other studies and what benefits they found from those resources.

Meanwhile, students with their own horses might be in need of *mounted* independent study. This would be attending a clinic or lesson with another instructor where you are *not* in attendance. Again, the same above rules apply. Recommend an instructor you respect; be sure they sign up for the proper level lesson and follow up on the results. Occasionally in the aftermath of such a lesson, some reading between the lines and positive interpretation will need to be done by you *for* your student to help reduce confusion or frustration. Not all clinics or lessons result in an immediate "light-bulb" experience; chin up!

AND LAST, FOR RECOMMENDING SABBATICAL TYPE INDEPENDENT STUDY OPPORTUNITIES, FOLLOW THE SAME ABOVE CHECKLIST, *PLUS* PREPARE YOUR STUDENT FOR THE UPCOMING TRANSITIONS THEY WILL .EXPERIENCE. Most sabbatical type periods go smoothly if your student meets few surprises and they overcome that initial "home-sickness" period. Make a point to see them off with your blessing and try to be available for console while they are away.

Chapter Five

INSTRUCTOR SKILLS

TIPS FOR CONDUCTING SAFETY CHECKS:

Safety checks are a fundamental ingredient for good teaching at *all* levels of riding. The earlier topic on safety focused on teaching students to be accountable for safety. This topic is devoted to the procedure in lessons that enables us to catch, or more often *prevent* unsafe conditions in terms of equipment: i.e. safety checks. Lets define a safety check to be the time an instructor spends on checking tack, rider apparel, facility equipment and so on. Basically, a safety check is an inspection. Conducting safety checks benefits *both* horses and riders in terms of reducing injuries. Additionally, the time an instructor spends on conducting a safety check is educational. For novice riders this involves providing *new information*; for intermediate students, *feedback is provided from the instructor to the student regarding the correctness of student preparations*; for advanced students, safety checks *identify the wide range of details* that contribute to safety.

BUILD YOUR CASE FOR SAFETY CHECKS. Enforcing safety standards and principles is one of the harder aspects that instructors face in teaching horsemanship. Fortunately, yet unfortunately, riders get away with unsafe practices every day. This entices individuals into sloppy habits around horses. Unfortunately, this grooms an environment for "accidents waiting to happen." Encouraging your students to get in habits that will serve them well during the *uncommon* yet *real situations* that lead to serious accidents takes a combination of persuasion, rules and education. One of the more valuable tactics is to set a good example yourself; however, this alone rarely *changes* students' behavior, except *after* an accident has happened. Preventing accidents is certainly our first choice, so the "ways and means" you choose to enforce your safety rules sets a standard.

SAFETY CHECKS FOR NEW RIDERS SHOULD BE DONE *BEFORE THESE RIDERS MOUNT.* While each program / instructor will have their own system for getting the horses ready, as well as defining what a safety check should entail, *this safety check should be done by the instructor just before the rider/s mount.* This exposes the student to the process; thus, beginning *their* education on checking for safety *before* mounting. Do not rush through safety checks, this time is valuable for horsemanship education. Develop a system which is efficient yet thorough. Providing information to these new students as you do your safety check is fundamental. As these new riders progress, an instructor should begin using the safety check time to quiz each student on their knowledge. Safety check games can be devised, these are fun and meaningful to student education. Rushing to get new students into the saddle at this level of riding wastes the opportunity to build horsemanship skills as well as increases the likelihood that the instructor will miss an important element that contributes to safety.

SAFETY CHECKS FOR INTERMEDIATE AND ADVANCED STUDENTS SHOULD EMPHASIZE FEEDBACK TO STUDENTS ON THEIR SKILL AND APPLICATION OF SAFETY KNOWLEDGE. Numerous effective strategies exist for these higher level students. Here are several useful examples: *Upon arrival into the ring*, ask the riders to switch horses and check their classmate's tack; what do they find? *After a short warm up at the walk*, announce you are doing a "spot" check for girth tightness; ask: "how tight do you think your girth is?" before it is physically checked. *Unannounced and about once a week*, inspect students' tack for detail areas such as: the stitching on girth, stirrup & bit connections - is any key stitching weak? Saddle pads - are they clean & comfortable for the horse? Stirrup pads - are they worn out? And so on.

While safety checks are our "formal" approach, **INFORMAL BUT EQUALLY IMPORTANT ARE "WIDE EYES" FOR SAFETY DURING A LESSON. WIDE EYES MEANS DETECTING POTENTIAL SAFETY HAZARDS DURING A LESSON.** Missing a gate, not shut properly by a student of your next lesson who came in with a quick question - *can happen.* What about the garden snake that just entered the ring and is causing the horses concern even before riders notice? Variables can and do change *during* a lesson; safety checks at the start of a lesson are just the beginning!

TIPS TO DEVELOP YOUR EYE AS AN INSTRUCTOR:

Talented instructors have an important teaching skill in common; they have developed an "eye" for evaluating the movement of the rider and horse. This "eye", appreciated by colleagues and clients, enables an instructor to identify the root of a problem and recognize minute skill changes in either the rider, the horse or both. An instructor's "eye" is also the foundation of providing feedback to the student regarding their progress. Although values, goals and curriculum shade differently the "eye" we develop, here are some fundamental tips that will help any instructor improve or sharpen their "eye."

WHERE POSSIBLE, AN INSTRUCTOR SHOULD USE STATIONARY ENVIRONMENTS SUCH AS THE HORSE STANDING STILL, A SAW HORSE OR SIMPLY THE RIDER ON THEIR OWN TWO FEET TO CLEARLY SEE RIDER MOVEMENT. Undesirable patterns of movement in the rider are not only easily detected in stationary environments, but also, the student can focus on the movement of their own body without the added motion of the horse. For example, a beginner student is having difficulty with posting to the trot. This student crouches forward, draws their legs up and gets behind the rhythm of the horse. Which position improvement will help the most? Which ones are secondary? While a horse is in motion, out of balance riders often lapse into many compensation errors that make it harder to see the root of their balance problem. By asking a student to post while the horse is standing still, an instructor will be able to identify or rule out those errors that relate to the motion of the trot. Discovery of details such as the rider *folds* forward fractional before they attempt to push upward are far more easily seen without the motion of the horse.

ANOTHER USEFUL TOOL FOR DEVELOPING YOUR 'EYE' IS WHERE YOU STAND IN THE RING. Particularly for lateral balance issues, moving from the center of the ring to a corner or a wall is needed. Determining if the rider's outside leg position is fueling their lateral balance problem, can be achieved by observing the outside leg or standing in front or behind the rider to compare their legs and hips. Another useful angle is the aerial view. Second story observation areas will achieve this view. The aerial view allows for assessing how much a rider is out of lateral *and* longitudinal balance at the same time. This view is very handy for helping those riders who collapse a hip. Furthermore, the aerial view enables us to best see the lateral balance and bending of the horse.

A WONDERFUL TOOL TO DEVELOP YOUR EYE IS VIDEO TAPING, Video taping enables an instructor to re-run parts of a lesson over and over. Looking for problem areas not caught while we are in the midst of teaching is made possible by this tool. Video also allows us a slow motion review. This feature is excellent for studying position relationships and the mechanical movement of the horse and rider. Yet review in regular speed is best for studying rhythm.

Last, **A HINT TO SHARE WITH YOUR STUDENTS IS HOW HELPFUL IT IS TO HAVE THEM DRESS IN CLOTHES AND COLORS THAT WILL HELP YOU DO YOUR JOB MORE EASILY.** Something as simple as tucking in a loose blouse will improve your ability to see correct posture. Wearing colors that contrast with the horse's color, brings out valuable details of rider position and aids. For training new instructors, it can be a real boost to have the horse wear different colored leg wraps on their diagonal pairs. This will help a new instructor speed up their recognition of correct or incorrect diagonals. Bless those horses that have natural marking achieving that same effect!

TIPS ON USING YOUR VOICE EFFECTIVELY:

Since conversation is a large portion of our teaching environment, how we use our voice contributes to the messages we are trying to communicate. Our students need to be able to hear what we are saying, understand what we are saying and have the time to process what has been said. Lets look at important tips for effective use of a riding instructor's voice:

THE TONES OF YOUR VOICE, EXPRESS MEANING. Tones of compassion *soothe;* tones of excitement *dance.* How we use tones to communicate, enables us to reduce how many words we need to express meaning. Mostly, a practicing rider receives our conversation without the assistance of body language to aid meaning. Therefore, *tones* and *diction* play a strong role for teachers of athletics. Rhythm, energy, flow, interruption, consistency, can all be described by tones and diction. Suzie, f l-o-a-t down to that oxer; Gary, you need to TELL Sprite you want him to turn left.....not ask him to turn left; Rhoda, that circle was *P E R F E C T.*

BREATHING DEEPLY TO TALK FROM THE DIAPHRAGM HELPS VOICE PROJECTION AND CLARITY. While we emphasize "breathing deeply" for students to gain or maintain elasticity and relaxation while riding; breathing deeply also enables an instructor to *project* their voice and to speak *distinctly* over the sizable spaces of riding rings and fields. Breathing deeply, then, using one's diaphragm to push the words out over the vocal cords serves to *project* ones' voice and saves on vocal cord strain. It is desirable to keep the pitch of your voice from becoming shrill when projecting across large areas because this reduces clarity. Mumbling, thick accents or talking rapidly also decreases the ability of students on moving horses to understand the words you are speaking. When students cannot hear, directions have to be repeated or confusion results. Over time, students who cannot hear are bound to get frustrated. We need to make our voices audible; however, if all the members of a lesson are able to hear easily, except one - check to be sure this student does not have a hearing loss problem.

UTILIZE ACOUSTICS THAT WILL HELP YOUR VOICE CARRY. Generally, there are advantages to the sound carriage of indoor rings. Indoor rings hold out neighboring sounds, while they also provide some inherent acoustics. Not all indoor arenas carry sound the same. Much will depend on the materials the walls are made of, the footing, the size of the ring (circumference and height) and the windows. Metal increases sound vibration; wood decreases sound vibration. This is because dense materials "reflect" sound waves while porous materials absorb sound waves. Outdoors, certain locations will provide natural acoustics. Valleys hold in sound; sides of buildings and thick tree lines can reverberate sound. These natural sound boosters are useful for lessons where a lot of teacher talk is needed while the student is in motion. Additionally, weather conditions such as a steady light wind, can help to carry your voice as you position yourself wind wisely.

Certain teaching conditions may require **EQUIPMENT THAT AMPLIFIES OR CARRIES YOUR VOICE.** Popular equipment includes: hand held megaphones; cordless mic's that amplify through speakers; cone horns; hands free wireless walkie talkie systems, etc. Megaphones and cordless mic's amplify and broadcast one's voice. These are useful for spreading your conversation over a larger space; however, this type of equipment also increases the "noise" level which might be unacceptable in your neighborhood. Cone horns (which do not require batteries) project one's voice without broadcasting. A cone horn points the amplification in *one* direction - quite useful for directing comments to individual riders. Hands free walkie-talkies allow for conversation back and forth between the instructor and student/s through headsets and mics. Cupping your hands around your mouth makes a miniature cone horn which helps when no equipment is handy!

LAST BUT NOT LEAST, *WHEN* **AN INSTRUCTOR USES THEIR VOICE, AS WELL AS HOW, INFLUENCES TEACHING.** Precise timing of vocal directions, aids the improvement of a rider's timing. No teacher talk, might be desirable when a student needs to concentrate on their practice, or the horse responds more quickly than the rider, and so on.

TIPS FOR PRESENTING MATERIAL CLEARLY:

One of the more challenging aspects of teaching is *how to* impart information, directions, exercises and philosophy in a manner which will be clear. Clarity starts with instructor organization. Clarity is achieved when the accuracy of material, meets the needs of the student. And last, presenting material clearly, improves with experience. Let us look at these three influences on clarity for horseback riding instruction.

CLARITY STARTS WITH INSTRUCTOR ORGANIZATION. For *horseback* riding instructors, our ability to provide instructional organization is fundamental to our personal command of horsemanship and those riding skills to be taught. Quality lesson plans, accurate student performance assessment, and successful curriculum progression can be achieved when the instructor possesses mastery of the equestrian studies to be taught. Following this, adequate preparation time is the next most influential component of instructor organization. Whether the lesson is a classroom lecture on bits and their influence, or a riding lesson on how to ride in an open field, preparation time enables the instructor to organize for clarity. This time is used to choose terminology, create strategic planning, conduct additional topic research, prepare resources for the lesson and troubleshoot elements to a presentation which might be ineffective. The last phase of instructor organization occurs during the lesson. Invariably, problems can occur during a lesson which might sway a lesson plan. In order to *present* material clearly, an instructor needs to navigate these conditions. Treating these problems as interruptions rather than *needs* will enable the instructor to stay on track. Furthermore, while it is always important to field student questions, presenting material draws upon a student's ability to *listen* and/or *observe*. Therefore, limiting student questions or asking students to hold their questions until the *end* of your presentation is advisable. Generally, most routine questions *are* answered by the conclusion of an effective presentation. Particularly for demonstration presentations, this observation time helps to build a student's *eye* for horsemanship and proper riding skills. Likewise, listening time during short lectures in a riding lesson, encourages a student to concentrate and engages them in *receiving* information.

NEXT, CLARITY IS ACHIEVED WHEN THE ACCURACY OF MATERIAL, MEETS THE NEEDS OF THE STUDENT. Let us look at two examples. Linda does not want to jump. She loves horses, but she simply does not have interest in jumping them. However correct and accurate jumping material is presented in terms of teaching/learning philosophy: Linda does not want to jump. While Linda's riding interests might later include jumping, sadly, it is downright improbable that a clear presentation for Linda, has been accomplished. George has been placed in a group of stronger riders to accommodate the car pooling needs of parents. The content of his lessons tend to fly over his head because he is not as advanced. Again, *clarity*, for George, is lost. In a nutshell, it is difficult to achieve *clarity* if the material is not suited to the needs of the student. Attention to student needs prevents our lectures and demonstrations from dwindling into a pontificating downward spiral or words lost to flying over one's head. Instead, clear presentations of material are achieved when close attention has been given to student needs which include: appropriate topic of material, appropriate difficulty, a reasonable quantity of information presented to the learner, and so on. But there is a caution here for horseback riding instructors, horsemanship needs for a student are not always reflected by the wants of that student or the wants of the instructor. For example in Linda's situation, perhaps she needs freedom to explore the various disciplines to find a participation with horses she favors. For George's situation, perhaps some degree of special attention is warranted so George receives instruction at his level of need. This could be accomplished by the presentation of material including a split level approach or during certain portions of George's lessons, he is separated from his group to receive the individual instruction he needs at his current level.

And last, **presenting material clearly, improves with experience.** i. e. instructor despair dwindles, etc. etc.

TIPS FOR EVALUATING A NEW STUDENT'S SKILLS:

When we get new students, the first step toward planning effective lessons, is to evaluate their background. New students will have either ridden previously or not. For both types of students, evaluating their existing athletic skills will help us to provide quality instruction. Lets look at these two rider profiles separately.

EVALUATING NEW STUDENTS' SKILLS: ***THOSE WHO HAVE NEVER RIDDEN.*** Gaining accurate background information on "new to riding" students, helps to define their *aptitude* for horseback riding. Furthermore, this information will shed some light on how quickly they will progress through your initial course of riding instruction. The following type of information will be useful:

- why do they want to learn & participate in horseback riding?
- how old are they? do they have any disabilities?
- how familiar are they with horses and/or other large animals?
- does their lifestyle include small animals, if so what kinds?
- how physically fit are they; strength (isotonic) & aerobics (endurance)?
- what other sports have they participated in? to what level? how long ago?

These are examples of useful information to obtain. Seeking information on skills that closely transfer to horseback riding will help to define your new student's *raw* potential. How other athletic activities size up in their similarity to riding - helps *a lot*. *Our* knowledge of related skills, particularly athletic skills (recreational or competitive), enables *us* to provide more effective instruction. For example, if a student has peddled a bike while turning, they know the sensations of moving the handlebar while coordinating peddling. These sensations and coordination requirements are very similar to steering and keeping a horse going forward for new riders. Comparisons that *closely transfer* are worth their weight in gold.

Meanwhile, obtaining background information through verbal interviews, written forms and simple *"skill tests"* is advisable. *Simple skill tests* can be accomplished through having common everyday sports equipment on hand. A bicycle, a skate board, a mini trampoline for example, will provide reliable insights on new students' present abilities including balance, coordination, attitude, confidence and so on. While some aspiring riders may have considerable previous athletic background - should that background be *10 years ago*, this is a different "new rider" compared to the active athlete.

EVALUATING NEW STUDENTS' SKILLS: ***THOSE WHO HAVE RIDDEN.*** The preceding strategies together with methods for assessing riding skills are all beneficial. While students' perceptions of their skill level may not coincide with yours, usually lack of agreement rests mostly in skill level definitions, rather than *"actual competencies"* for specific riding skills. Therefore, determining *actual skill competencies* through questions and mounted exercises will be efficient, accurate as well as friendly. To develop verbal or written questions that reveal skill competencies, first identify and list specific riding skills. Then create *degrees of mastery* for those skills; include: *1) ability to perform 2) frequency and context 3) ease.* For example, you are developing a questionnaire for new students who declare they are an intermediate. One questions is: When picking up the canter: circle all answers that apply:

- you determine your lead by looking at the shoulders, sometimes
- you determine your lead by looking at the shoulders, all the time
- you can feel your lead, sometimes on certain horses
- you can feel your lead, sometimes on all horses
- you can feel your lead, all the time on certain horses
- you can feel your lead, if given the time to concentrate, on all horses
- easily, you can feel your lead, all the time, on all horses
- _____ (a choice you feel is missing)

Which responses a new student chooses and any response they contribute will help to define their riding abilities. *In a similar fashion*, develop your *mounted* skill evaluation exercises to include these basic components of: *1) ability to perform 2) frequency and context 3) ease.* Good questionnaires and mounted evaluation lessons take time to cultivate. Custom make your evaluation tools to suit your clientele and program. Then, be sure to modify your tools over time until you have a reliable system established.

TIPS TO DETERMINE STUDENT LEARNING:

Our sensitivity, observation and acknowledgment of student learning, plays a large role in teaching. Determining student learning can be a labor of love or a nightmare. An instructor's "mental black book" contains many notations of progress, both favorable and unfavorable. In a way, we become "scorekeepers" of our student's progress. Naturally, "leaps" in learning are far easier to recognize than minute changes for students as well as instructors. Some learning is physical in nature, such as, being able to stretch one's heels downward or coordinating rein and leg aids properly. While other learning accomplishments are more invisible, such as, diminishing fear or gaining an increased appreciation for a particular riding principle. For sure, *unnoticed* progress will haunt an instructor. The results are: a deterioration of communication with the student and a tendency to hold the student back. Conversely, overrating a student's abilities creates low achievement standards and safety problems. Lets look at some sound measures for determining student learning:

THE CLICHÉ, "WE LEARN BY DOING" IS A VERY VALUABLE TECHNIQUE *INSTRUCTORS* CAN USE WHEN IT COMES TO DETERMINING STUDENT LEARNING. Wrapping up a lesson with a final exercise; giving a rider the chance to graduate from a "schooled mount" to a greener mount; inviting a rider to demonstrate certain skills for an elementary class; taking a student to a horse show; taking a student off the lunge line, are a few, of the *many* examples of "doing" things we can ask our students to perform which will shed light on just how much they have learned. Essentially, asking a student to *use* their skills under somewhat different conditions will create friendly and informal tests which will help you measure students' progress.

THERE IS A DIFFERENCE BETWEEN DETERMINING *STUDENT LEARNING* AND DETERMINING *STUDENT PERFORMANCE*, BE-CAUSE LEARNING AND PERFORMANCE ARE NOT ALWAYS SYN-ONYMOUS. For teaching leisure or competitive sports, this principle holds very true. One example would be: a student who rarely has difficulty keeping their legs in the proper position, is having a "bad day"...... resulting from too little sleep the night before. Furthermore, they came to your lesson having ridden three horses beforehand. The bottom line is: *they are physically tired.* Their *performance* may not be "up to par" but they can still *learn* (mentally and physically) from the exercises of your lesson as long as the conditions are not dangerous and their fatigue does not escalate to exhaustion. Check their *performance* during their next lesson .... and advise them to come more rested.

QUESTIONS AND DIALOGUE ARE POPULAR TECHNIQUES USED TO DETERMINE STUDENT LEARNING; THEY ARE BEST COMBINED WITH INSTRUCTOR FEEDBACK ON *ACTUAL* PERFORMANCE. This combination provides an objective determination of learning. Ideal times for questions and dialogue are promptly following practice sessions or in combination with video re-runs of practice. Do not assess *performance* strictly through dialogue. During a horse show, asking your student how their last western riding pattern went (you were watching another student scheduled in a different ring) will shed light on what your student has learned, but only *some* light on their performance. Exciting new discoveries or unusual difficulties tend to shade students' self- assessment. Student assessed highs and lows, need to be blended into *your* evaluation. Continuing the dialogue with a question like this will help: "Now Susie, I understand you felt your pattern was erratic. Can you compare *how* erratic it was to the first pattern you did in our last lesson at home?" This additional information will help create a closer picture of their actual performance of the pattern.

DETERMINING STUDENT LEARNING IS AN *ONGOING* PROCESS INVOLVED IN YOUR DAILY LESSONS. Most importantly, these measures, enable us to proceed with lesson plans that suit our students.

TIPS TO KEEP CRITICISMS CONSTRUCTIVE AND POSITIVE:

In teaching horseback riding, we criticize our students to help them progress faster. Random House Dictionary defines criticize as: to make judgments as to merit (of); to find fault (with); blame, censure, condemn. Certainly if we come across as blaming, censuring or condemning, we will not get very far. But if we can share judgments and identify faults in a positive and constructive manner, our criticisms will be very welcomed by students. Lets examine three axioms for making criticisms positive and constructive to improve the flow of our lessons.

First, WHEN YOU IDENTIFY A PROBLEM TO YOUR STUDENTS, IDENTIFY A SOLUTION AS WELL. For example, Susie is told she is posting too high out of the saddle. One instructor might suggest that Susie keep some bend in her knees as she posts up rather than completely straightening her leg. While another instructor might suggest that Susie try to "soften" her post which will result in less height to her posting. Both suggestions offer a *solution* for Susie to try. Sounds simple and it is simple. But as the complexity of our lessons evolve, it can be dangerously easy to not fulfill this simple axiom. For example, in some lessons we want our students to experiment and come up with a solution themselves. When this is your strategy, be sure to *tell* the students you are encouraging them to seek a solution. Leaving out permission or encouragement for the student to seek out the solution would result in your teaching being critical and no solution offered.

Secondly, to keep criticism constructive and positive, RECOGNIZE IMPROVEMENT AS YOUR STUDENTS ARE BUILDING NEW SKILLS. Do not wait for the skill to be completely accomplished before you provide positive feedback. Put yourself in the riding ring. Today's group lesson is on getting some flexion to the bit and improving the horse's longitudinal balance. These students are intermediate level riders on greener horses. They can accomplish this skill on schooled horses, but are now learning how to teach greener horses about flexion and getting off the forehand. "Henry, that is not enough response to your aids to get Poco to improve his longitudinal balance, however, you have accomplished some softening in his jaw - that is a solid beginning, good job!" When we recognize small improvements, this guides learning toward the bigger accomplishments. Thus, motivation and patience are cultivated in our students. While realizing there is yet more to accomplish, this dialogue pointed out to Henry that he had accomplished a foundation step: Poco softening his jaw. Now, listen to the dialogue without the positive and constructive comments: "Henry, that is not enough response to your aids to get Poco to improve his longitudinal balance." This type feedback for an entire lesson or longer would certainly result in frustration for Henry.

Last, criticizing a student's "feel" is perhaps the most tenuous subject there is in teaching horseback riding. **USE DIRECTING A STUDENT TO INCREASE OR DECREASE THEIR PRESENT FEEL, FOR GUIDING THEM TO ACHIEVE A MORE CORRECT "FEEL."** Nothing is worse from the students standpoint of view, than to be informed that they have "the wrong feel." It is one thing if a student comes to you and expresses that they know something feels wrong. It is yet another to be told they "have the wrong feel or that they don't feel it." This launches the student into a vast unknown. What will the correct feel, feel like? When will they feel it? How will they know when they have it? We all know these questions are very hard to answer. Analogies that your students can relate to will be helpful, but still they need our help with *their* feel. Avoid telling your student they have the wrong feel, but instead give your student a measure of what they *do* feel, to change. For example: "Susie, to obtain a more desirable lighter rein contact, take your present feel of the reins and reduce it by 25%. After you practice for a few minutes to accomplish this, I'll let you know if that amount is enough." This modulation, increasing or decreasing their present feel, will yield meaningful new sensations for the student. Work with your students' feel - it works!

TIPS FOR GIVING COMPLIMENTS:

Let us divide giving compliments into three different occurrences:

- *complimenting a student's practice*
- *complimenting the student with positive talk, and*
- *compliments paid to a student which identify a student's incremental progress*

Probably the most deciding factor about giving compliments in the realm of teaching, is that the *student* feels complimented. If you have tried to give your horseback riding student a compliment, yet they do not *feel* complimented, rework your approach. Now, let us look at these three different aspects of giving compliments.

COMPLIMENTING A STUDENT'S HORSEBACK RIDING MEANS PROVIDING POSITIVE FEEDBACK ABOUT THEIR PRACTICE. Specifically this refers to when an instructor tells the student they are performing the skill *correctly*; conversely, giving negative feedback refers to when an instructor tells the student they are performing the skill *incorrectly*. Most experts in physical education stress that all feedback (both positive and negative) should be delivered in a positive manner. Furthermore, both types of feedback can either be immediate or delayed. Students' knowledge of practice results, hence instructor feedback, helps to mold students' future practice. Feedback given in a testing manner, can help instructors determine student cognition and horsemanship "feel." For example, providing a student the feedback that they have the proper diagonal (which they do), yet eluding to maybe they don't by frowning, and then asking them "are you *s u r e?*", can help to reveal students who are "second guessing." Should feedback given in a testing manner reveal a student IS guessing, instructors need to promptly reinforce *to* the student, what *is* correct. Beware of negative feedback given in a negative manner; this approach generally creates chaos. It is more desirable to withhold negative feedback until this feedback can be presented in a positive fashion. Rarely do instructors present negative feedback in a negative manner, because the result tends to be more punishing than instructional. Nonetheless and unfortunately, this circumstance can occur if a student responds negatively to negative feedback. Should a student become angry because of negative feedback provided, care should be taken that the horse not be caught in the cross fire and the student's anger addressed.

COMPLIMENTING THE STUDENT WITH POSITIVE TALK MEANS TALKING POSITIVELY OR PLACING A NEGATIVE SITUATION IN A

POSITIVE LIGHT. While positive talk is certainly desirable and vastly more comfortable for students and instructors alike, there are limits to "positive" talk. Endless positive "talk" runs thin on value, resulting in *just* "talk." Put yourself in the ring setting. Harry and Anne take a semi-private lesson weekly. They are intermediate level riders, nearing advanced level horseback riding skills. They are both eager to make that advancement. Meanwhile, their instructor has been providing little, except compliments during their recent practice. The result: little skill advancement. Thus, for instruction, "positive talk" walks a thin line between the delicate balance of compliments and challenges. Now return to the horseback ring setting. As a result of little recent skill progress, the instructor decides it is time to challenge Harry and Anne; thus their game of pole bending gets timed against the clock. Whoever is fastest on the clock wins that game. Meanwhile, both students emerge winners because the looser of that game receives information on how to improve - thus *instruction* places loosing, in a positive light.

COMPLIMENTS PAID TO A STUDENT WHICH IDENTIFY A STUDENT'S INCREMENTAL PROGRESS, REPRESENT A TIME TO CELEBRATE! Plus, these compliments are occasional. As horseback riding instructors plan their curriculum, students *should* be aware of when they have moved up a grade level. Another words, they have put another notch on their totem pole. While the end of a set period of time does not necessarily indicate this skill progress success, achievement does. Because some students will progress faster than others, take care in providing incremental progress recognition. Remain sensitive to any student who feels "left behind" and continue to offer guidance of how they too, can progress their riding skills.

TIPS FOR QUESTIONING TECHNIQUES:

Verbal questions serve many purposes for the teaching-learning process. Both instructors and students ask and receive questions. Developing diverse questioning techniques takes study, practice and exploration. Questions yield us information. Questions provide an avenue for student participation. Questions identify future needs for learning. When an instructor closes a lesson with "are there any questions?" less meaningful questions result. Rather, questions which are a *part* of our lessons provide the most useful and tangible results.

PRINCIPALLY, INSTRUCTORS USE VERBAL QUESTIONS TO DETERMINE AND GUIDE STUDENT LEARNING. Benjamin Bloom formulated six levels of human thinking/ reasoning into a taxonomy of the cognitive domain (Educational Objectives, Handbook I, 1956). They are:

1) knowledge ..... which progresses to...... 2) comprehension .... which progresses to...
3) application ... which progresses to.... 4) analysis ..... which progresses to......
5) synthesis ..... then finalizes in...... 6) evaluation ...... the highest level

How instructors formulate questions will lean toward one of these levels of cognition. Questions which ask a rider to remember or identify what they know are *knowledge level* questions; the most basic level. Questions which ask a rider to explain, describe or summarize, are *comprehension level* questions. Questions which ask a rider to apply or demonstrate what they have learned are *application level* questions. Questions which ask a rider to analyze and identify relationships are *analysis level* questions. Questions which ask a rider to create or suppose are *synthesis level* questions. And last, questions which ask a rider for their judgment, opinion, expertise, etc. are *evaluation level* questions.

While answers to cognitive questions will not always reflect riding skill abilities, *students' answers* to cognitive questions will identify the lacking ingredients of knowing and/or perceiving which in turn influence skill abilities. Furthermore, student answers to cognitive questions can also identify when the progress needed, is strictly "skill related" and not theory based. Now, put yourself in the ring. Susie is having difficulty learning about half halts. She can recite your definition of what a half halt is inside and out - yet she still is unable to determine when she has achieved one, except when being coached stride by stride. You ask her: "Under what conditions would you use a half halt?" Again, she replies with all the correct answers. As your questions and her answers progress, you discover she can even readily see and determine when *other* riders should have applied a half halt, or when they failed to obtain a half halt they asked for. Your questions and Susie's answers have identified that Susie thoroughly *understands* half halts to the highest level of cognition. Now, she simply needs to achieve them physically. Susie's next several lessons will certainly center on practice, practice, practice! Conversely, George is having difficulty in getting his horse to turn, precisely when he asks. Usually his horse has a delayed reaction. When you ask George: "how strong have your half halts been before you turn?" George looks bewildered, "half halts," he responds, sheepishly "should I be using half halts before I turn?" While George knows how to give a half halt, George obviously does not know *all of the conditions* for which half halts are useful. This encounter, and George's new knowledge gained, will help guide his cognition of half halts from the application level to the analysis level. A meaningful discovery for both student and instructor.

WHEN INSTRUCTORS ASK QUESTIONS THAT PROVOKE DEBATE AND STUDENT EXPLORATION, HIGHER LEVELS OF COGNITION RESULT. Instructors do not always have all the answers. Additionally, for complex problems, several different resolutions may satisfy the same problem. Thus, when instructors encourage debate and student exploration through questions which are, in a sense, "unanswered," a healthy challenge has been set into motion.

AND LAST, WHEN STUDENTS ASK US QUESTIONS, WE ARE PROVIDED THE SAME OPPORTUNITY TO ASSESS AND PROGRESS COGNITION. Furthermore, student initiated questions have a high level of student involvement, they are worth their weight in gold!

TIPS TO VARY HOW WE PROVIDE STUDENTS FEEDBACK:

My research during the mid- 1980's on the teaching methods (behaviors) of expert riding instructors reveals that horseback riding instructors value providing feedback *immediately*. They critique the desirable and undesirable parts of student practice and suggest how to improve future practice attempts. This research also revealed that horseback riding instructors do not tend to use methods of delaying feedback to the student when teaching a new motor skill. These instructors also valued video tape feedback for riding instruction but infrequently used this method of providing feedback to the learner.

MOST PHYSICAL EDUCATORS DISTINGUISH BETWEEN TWO ORIGINS OF FEEDBACK FOR THE LEARNER: INTERNAL AND EXTERNAL. Internal feedback is the information generated by a person's kinesthetic sense residing in muscles, joints and tendons. Whereas, external feedback gives information to the learner while the skill is occurring. The learner's external sensory organs of sight, hearing, touch, taste and smell provide the feedback rather than the action itself. Researchers DeCecco and Crawford identify two main types of external feedback: intrinsic and extrinsic. Intrinsic feedback refers to knowledge of the results which are *perceived by the learner* from the task itself or the consequences of the learner's actions. For example: a rider seeing they have rounded a barrel without knocking it over during barrel racing. Whereas, extrinsic feedback refers to knowledge of the results provided by an *external source* to the learner and external to the task being performed. This type of feedback is principally given by the teacher, the horse and other observers. We, the instructors, need to account for both the intrinsic and extrinsic aspects of external feedback in our lesson planning. Meanwhile as our students progress, *their* internal feedback will develop as their skills become naturalized enabling them to be less and less dependent on external sources for feedback. In a nutshell, their "feel" blossoms.

BE SURE TO PROVIDE TIME IN LESSONS FOR STUDENTS TO ASSESS THEIR INTRINSIC FEEDBACK. Since we are the "experts", it is easy to supply extrinsic feedback and neglect providing time for students to perceive intrinsic feedback through their senses. Students *using* their external senses to perceive and evaluate personal performance is a building block toward cultivating the internal feedback system....or their "feel." Thus, too much teacher talk can become a barrier to student learning. For example: John is working on getting his leg longer. Following a certain period of work, his instructor asks him to evaluate his performance in this area. John shares that he can tell when he starts to draw his legs up because the skirts of his saddle start making a soft flapping noise as he grips too much rather than stretches down sufficiently. This noise reminds him to stretch his legs down. He has noticed that this coincides with the instructor's feedback about his legs. In this example of John's, he shared an "intrinsic" feedback system *he* discovered. While in other cases, it is helpful for the instructor to suggest an intrinsic measure for students to use. For example: "Susie, each time you pass the mirror on either side of the ring, check your leg length in the mirror." Then, our job becomes leaving *time* for Susie to carry out this task.

BE CREATIVE ABOUT PROVIDING EXTRINSIC FEEDBACK TO YOUR STUDENTS. INCLUDE THE HORSE, OTHER STUDENTS, AND OBSERVERS IN THIS PROCESS. Some useful examples are: Randy, if you are pinching too much with your legs, Trigger tends to back his ears in objection - look for this. Sally, where did Sheila's leg go during her last time through the gymnastic? Mrs. Hunt, is Henry's posture on horseback better or worse than his posture at home?

LAST, THERE IS SOMETHING MAGICAL ABOUT USING PICTURES AND VIDEOS OF YOUR STUDENTS TO PROVIDE PERFORMANCE FEEDBACK. Use them; they are well worth working into your repertoire!

Chapter Six

INSTRUCTOR STRATEGIES

TIPS TO IMPROVE COMMUNICATION IN YOUR LESSONS:

Communication in our lessons can range from the vocabulary we use, to the methods we choose to determine how much our students have learned. Improving our communication means taking a look at how we operate in our lessons. How do we communicate with our students? How do we encourage our students to communicate with us? Here are two ideas that should help.

An instructor spends a good deal of time defining terms so a student can learn our varied and sometimes foreign "horse jargon." **BUT MANY POPULAR TERMS WITH INSTRUCTORS ALSO NEED TO BE REDEFINED AS A STUDENT PROGRESSES.** Definitions appropriate for beginners should be limited and more generalized. Then, as the student progresses, the instructor should encourage the student to expand their definitions. For example: In one fashion or another, beginners are taught about the horse's balance being on the forehand or off the forehand. Then, as the student progresses in experiencing these sensations on horseback together with gaining a greater understanding of conformation and locomotion, their definition of this concept will evolve. We, the instructors, play a significant role in helping a student relate particularly, sensations and movement, to the definitions of complex riding principles. The instructor who encourages their students to identify, analyze, compare and evaluate will have fewer problems with student confusion while definitions are, in a sense, gaining new meanings. This means leave time in your lessons for this type of conversation. Asking "are there any questions" at the conclusion of your lesson is not enough.

Instead, choose activities that will encourage discussion that results in your students identifying, analyzing, comparing or evaluating during a lesson. For example, you are planning to have the students of a group lesson practice a simple jumping course. Since this is an individual activity, you can also ask the other students to study each classmates' course and decide if the jump was "on the forehand" or "off the forehand." Their answers contribute to your evaluation of both student practice and peer observation. Stimulating student study can also be achieved by assigning homework. Think of all the learning value gained by a student who has been asked to select two pictures from their home library to bring to their next lesson. Looking for the best pictures they can find of a horse clearly on the forehand as opposed to off the forehand helps the student apply their definition. No matter what approach you choose, our students need our feedback on how correct they are in continuing to re-define definitions of complex riding principles.

Instructors also spend a good deal of time providing feedback to the student about how correct their riding skills are during practice. **THE STUDENT'S PROGRESS WILL BE FASTEST WHEN THEY UNDERSTAND BOTH THE INSTRUCTOR'S LANGUAGE AND WHAT, EXACTLY, THE INSTRUCTOR IS CRITIQUING.** Put yourself in a ring setting. Your student is in middle of practicing slowing down their young enthusiastic horse's jog trot. Your emphasis has been to identify the proper amount of slowness reasonable to ask for, at this point of the horse's training. "Yes that is slow enough....... yes try to maintain that ...... ooh your loosing it a little, no....... slow down... more.. yes ..... slow, slow.... This is called PROMPTING. Eventually the instructors reduces the words to something as simple as "yes/no" while the student is practicing. Progress is being made. Then, the instructor notices the student is using too much hand to slow the horse down rather than seat. So work begins on this as well. But the instructor does NOT choose different prompting words for the new subject matter. As the student continues to practice, the instructor says, no ..., no..... (meaning not enough seat). But, the student starts to get somewhat confused . "Is the instructor referring to my seat or the horse's pace?" It is necessary to use different prompting language such as "seat" to prompt additional areas of instruction. Prompting is a powerful teaching tool, however, be sure your students remain clear on WHAT you are prompting.

TIPS TO AVOID STUDENT BOREDOM:

With horseback riding as with other leisure and competitive sports, there is a great need on the part of the participant to enjoy the sport. The Random House dictionary defines boring as: 1) to weary by dullness, tedious repetition, etc. 2) a dull tiresome person, thing, etc. Synonyms are: fatigue, tire, annoy.

When we turn to the riding arena, common reasons for student boredom are: repetitious lesson plans; the subject of the lesson is lacking appeal to the student; lesson plans that fail to challenge the student; an instructor's delivery not adapted to the learning style of the student or a high student-instructor ratio class poorly managed. Although there is equal responsibility on a student's shoulders for applying themselves to any lesson at hand (after all the student is the one doing the learning), the ART of teaching fundamentally *means*, we should capture our students attention, develop lesson plans which will be fun for our students and encourage students to strive for higher goals; these measures are natural antidotes for boredom. Now, lets examine these three antidotes individually.

CAPTURING STUDENTS' ATTENTION BOILS DOWN TO STUDENT INVOLVEMENT. TRY LESSON APPROACHES THAT WILL INCLUDE BORED STUDENTS IN LESSON PLAN DECISIONS. When students take part in the decision making process of your lesson plans, they become more involved and more interested. For example: George likes horses but treats them a bit like a bicycle. Class activities are not fun unless there is action going on. Therefore anytime he is not actively riding, he is bored. He does not listen well and he does not relate to the horse as an animal friend. George needs to improve his listening skills and he also needs to develop a rapport with his horse. His instructor creatively involves him in this way: "George, identify which human friend's personality is most similar to your horse." George has to think for a while, then he replies, "Sam, my cousin." The instructor continues, "now, during all my lesson lectures, I want you to listen closely on behalf of your horse friend, who is like Sam but cannot speak. If you feel your his horse will not understand an exercise we are preparing for or if the exercise will be too easy, please speak up on behalf of your horse." George has been encouraged to represent his horse's point of view. As George speaks up on behalf of his horse, he will have an influence on the lesson plan decisions of increasing or decreasing the difficulty of the exercises to be practiced for his horse.

"FUN" LESSON PLANS WILL TAKE ON MANY DIFFERENT APPEARANCES. Some teachers have a knack for entertaining their students, while others are blessed with marvelous humor or sharp whit. Some teachers have a sixth sense for how to challenge a student without over facing them. Other teachers intuitively appeal to a student's deep interests. Regardless of the teacher's approach, the result of a lesson that has successfully combated boredom is the *student had fun*. Since different people have fun different ways, a fool proof method is to go straight to the source. Asking key questions of your students such as these will help: What exercises or activities do you enjoy the most? Have you had a lesson you found particularly humorous? Is there a lesson you would like to repeat? Rate your last lesson with a scale of 0-10 for how much fun you had.

And last, **WHEN STUDENTS STRIVE FOR HIGHER GOALS, THEY MAKE A COMMITMENT TO INCREASE THEIR LEARNING WHICH BRINGS ABOUT INCREASED MOTIVATION.** Students who are bored have accepted a lower standard. Healthy environments that help elevate goals are: rubbing elbows with role models, being involved in a "team spirit" effort, getting dazzled by a great performance, being challenged by friendly competition. Wise instructors bolster these environments which have the potential to eliminate boredom!

TIPS FOR CREATING LESSON CONTESTS:

Contests, for horseback riding lessons, are a way to settle the stream of new information we provide to our students. Principally, lesson contests ask a student to put skills they have a command of ..... to use! Thus, a little different than practicing a skill, to perfect that skill, contests provide the challenge of competition. Lesson contests are generally geared to be friendly and are often synonymous with games. Contests provide amusement, varying degrees of chance and often ask the participants to create strategies. Therefore, lessons' contests are valuable for maintaining a plateau of learning for the object of strengthening skills. Meanwhile, for our students, contests are fun and often a highlight. Here are some ideas for creating contests.

UTILIZE A LULL OF INTEREST ON YOUR STUDENT'S PART, AS AN OPPORTUNITY TO CREATE A LESSON CONTEST. Most often, a lull of interest in students, simply means they do not feel challenged enough. While challenging students with more difficult curriculum can answer this dilemma in some cases, more often, these students need to put their present abilities to a measure. Contests serve this niche perfectly. For example: A group of your students have been studying and practicing how to make a circle *perfectly* round. While you realize their circles still have some improvement yet needed, your students are getting bored with circles. Perhaps some of the lack of quality in their circles is connected to this boredom. Instead of switching to an entirely different exercise, you decide to create a circle *CONTEST*. From this group of students you ask for a volunteer to judge a circle *contest*. Next, you ask the remaining riders to decide upon how many circles will be judged. This group decides three circles each will be fair and square to determine who made the best *r o u n d* circles of the day. While the student judge puts their horse away in the barn (in preparation for judging the contest), the remaining riders are allowed to practice just a few more minutes. Meanwhile, you devise the judging parameters and the prize. With the judge ready for duty, you announce these details. The first two circles each rider makes will be one at a time. The size will be a quarter width of the arena; the size they have been perfecting during their last several lessons. Individually, each rider is to trot once around the ring first, then on their second trot around the ring, make a circle, one quarter width of the ring, half way down each long side. Secondly, with all riders trotting in a file - two horse lengths apart, the riders will be asked to make the third circle, same size, on the count of three from the judge. The prize for winning the best *r o u n d* circles of the day will be a hand shake of congratulations by each rider, judge and instructor at the end of the lesson!

A LESSON CONTEST, PLANNED AHEAD, CAN KICK-OFF THAT WEEK'S LESSONS TOWARD IMPROVING A PARTICULAR SKILL. For example: You have a particular student returning to you for a week of private lessons this spring. They have been unable to ride over the winter. At the closure of their fall lessons, they were gaining solid skills at sitting the trot. For this week's to lessons, you devise a small personal skill "contest." When ready to practice sitting the trot on day one, you produce a piece of paper the size of a dollar bill. This piece of paper is placed in the center of the seat of the saddle. Your rider is now informed of your contest: "Lets see *how long* you can keep this piece of paper from drifting out from under your seat when you practice sitting the trot." This "personal contest" is repeated the next day, and the next, and the next. By the last day of the week, this personal contest has taken shape. The prize: one of your farm trinkets for each day the paper bill is held. If needed, a good spirited consolation prize is given on the last day, for the longest ride the paper bill was held.

SOLICIT CONTEST IDEAS FROM YOUR STUDENTS, THEIR FAMILY AND FRIENDS. Just the very notion of a *CONTEST* brews imagination for auditors and students alike. Asking those individuals who observe your lessons as well as lesson members to contribute "contest" ideas, can be fresh and fruitful. Be prepared to adjust the contest details to suit the instructional needs of your students. While all ideas contributed are valuable, some will undoubtedly be more appropriate than others. Be tactful and organize suitable ideas for action!

TIPS FOR BEING TEACHING CREATIVE IN COLD WEATHER:

First and foremost, instructors need to manage the elements during cold weather. Encourage your students to wear proper clothing which is safe and warm. The horses also need a proper clip for their level of work and blanketing. Furthermore, be as flexible as possible with times and locations of lessons. A few hours can make quite a difference in temperature and footing, while a suitable riding space that is out of the wind is far less cold. If you do not have an indoor, planting some pine trees for a wind block around your riding ring or even parking large equipment where it can block the wind will help. After managing the elements, the next step is to be teaching creative with your lesson plans.... here are some ideas.

Being teaching creative in cold weather, mostly boils down to doing some solid lesson planning in advance. **TRY STARTING YOUR LESSON WITH AN ACTIVITY IN THE BARN OR ARENA WHICH WILL WARM UP YOUR RIDERS AND HORSES *BEFORE* THE RIDERS MOUNT.** For example, vigorous grooming instead of dusting the horse off, will get both the horse and rider's blood flowing. Once a rider *can groom*, the tendency is to disconnect the subject of grooming from our lessons. Occasionally, including grooming in a lesson even with advanced riders will prove to be very informative as many riders get quite slack about doing thorough grooming except to get the horse clean for special occasions. Particularly currying helps the rider warm up and should be done alternating their arms. Meanwhile the horse gets a healthy body massage from currying. Additionally deep muscle massage, TTeam and stretching exercises for the horse are becoming quite popular. Exposing your students to these areas of horse care and encouraging their application will be very helpful to reduce the toll of cold weather when horses are often stabled more and tend to move around less in the pasture. Another activity to warm up your riders and horses before they mount is to work on *proper leading* at the walk *and* trot. Much like grooming, proper leading falls by the wayside all too often. Having your students walk and trot for five to ten minutes, working on the horse's transitions and responses to the handler accomplishes physical warmth and beautifully establishes attention and concentration of horses and riders *prior* to riding. This can be helpful in putting more control in the rider's hands; very desirable when the horses are apt to be fresh. Unlike lunging, leading will warm the rider up as well as the horse and can be done with group lessons.

Once mounted, **UNTIL YOUR RIDERS ARE FULLY WARMED UP FROM EXERCISING, AVOID HAVING YOUR STUDENTS STAND OR WALK SO YOU CAN THEORIZE DURING THE BEGINNING OF A LESSON.** Instead, promptly begin your lessons with familiar exercises and activities where explanations and demonstrations are kept to a minimum. Focus on increasing the quality your rider's *existing* skills at the start of your lessons; this puts the beginning of your lesson *in motion*. Once your students are fully warmed up, relatively short periods of time can be devoted to explanations and demonstrations to introduce new material. Be ready to table student theory questions that turn into a "debate" until a warmer environment can be had, such as the lounge once the horses are put away. Remembering to keep rest and lectures short will keep fingers and toes warmer; thank goodness horses do not suffer with these extremities!

PROVIDING UNMOUNTED LESSONS FOR DAYS WHEN IT IS UNREASONABLE FOR RIDERS AND HORSES TO FARE THE ELEMENTS HAS GREAT VALUE. Classroom lectures, discussions, video tape reviews, rider unmounted exercise routines and so on, are a part of any rider's education. New riding skills can be introduced through careful selection of video footage. Critiquing video footage of your students provides endless possibilities. Choosing floor exercises that will strengthen your students' weak areas, provides them wonderful homework that pays off even in warm weather. Do not underestimate the value of unmounted lessons and neither should your students!

TIPS FOR COMPETITION PREPARATIONS:

For competitors and their coaches alike, there are two distinct plans while participating in competitions: to gain e x p e r i e n c e *or* aiming to w i n . Instructors who do the best job of coaching, prepare their students with guidance for which plan is most realistic and desirable at *that* point in time. Meanwhile, seasoned coaches show their strips by being ready with appropriate follow up lessons at home, should the outcome of the competition be vastly different from what the competitor and coach anticipated.

For equestrian competitions, most riders train at home with the same person who coaches them at competitions; *this IS most ideal.* Therefore, many riding instructors combine teaching roles with coaching roles because many horseback riders enjoy competing. While, some horseback riding instructors/coaches are much more competitive (about winning) than others, the fact is, *ONE* winner emerges. So, even the most "competitive" coach knows a lot about loosing too! Thus, few riders lack sportsmanship lessons, if they compete. Now, lets look at tips for properly preparing students for competitions.

PREPARING STUDENTS FOR GAINING COMPETITION E X P E R I E N C E MEANS THE COMPETITOR SHOULD BE FULLY PREPARED TO PERFORM THE TESTS FORTHCOMING, BUT NOT ENCOURAGED TO "GO FOR BROKE." Instructors who prepare their students properly will *not* face their competitors with *new* challenges during the competition they are entering. Thus a student should have practiced *all* the competition questions and tests at home - *beforehand.* When the exercises are familiar, gaining competition e x p e r i e n c e is successful. In a nutshell, the student is simply practicing while in a competition environment. Many coaches will describe this as "we are going for the mileage." Following a competition entered for gaining e x p e r i e n c e, keep your criticisms limited .... even the constructive ones. Encourage your students to evaluate their performance as compared to how they have performed at home in the past. Refrain from *and* discourage the comparing of their performance to the other competitors'; this helps to emphasize the "mileage" goal.

PREPARING STUDENTS FOR WINNING MEANS CHALLENGING YOUR STUDENT AT HOME TO *PERFECT* THEIR SKILLS TO A LEVEL WHICH WILL ENABLE THEM TO WIN IN A "COMPETITIVE" ENVIRONMENT. Imagine your student enters and wins a competition well below their skill and confidence level; this boarders on improper and questionable sportsmanship. Imagine your student enters and wins a small class where they have been the best of the worst on that day; this is really competition *experience*. But when a competitor wins fair and square and they have been challenged to win...... this is winning. In some circumstances, f i n i s h i n g *IS* w i n n i n g. A budding western stock seat competitor who makes the first cut but doesn't make the second cut at the QH Congress, is still a winner. An Eventing competitor who finishes our Rolex CCI **** Three Day Event, even *last*, is still a winner. Much depends on the level of difficulty of the tests, the quality of competitors, plus the luck of the day.

When an instructor is preparing a student to aim for w i n n i n g a competition, first the student must *feel* ready; both in terms of physical skills and confidence. Often preparations can be so demanding that any lack of desire will sink their chances long before you get them to the competition itself. In other words, be sure the student has signed, sealed and delivered their stamp of approval for aiming "to win." Next, the student must be capable of evaluating their failures at winning with a vigor to improve toward the next competition...... even if they felt they rode their best. Realistically - aiming to win with impressive preparations and a good dose of luck might *still* result in a fourth place finish. Constructive criticisms of how these other three competitors managed to beat your student, *n o w* will be helpful. Also identify why they beat the remaining competitors. Thus, this *IS* the time to encourage relating their performance to the other competitors'. Avoid excessive evaluation of why their particular performance was not good enough to win; that approach adds to their disappointment. And last, *should* your student win, ENJOY IT and CELEBRATE!

TIPS FOR COACHING AT A COMPETITION:

Naturally all riding instructors will have their own teaching and coaching styles; however, assisting a competitor *IS* different than striving to teach a new skill to a student or helping to perfect a student's existing skills. While most competitors and coaches would be thrilled to win frequently and *some* certainly do, competitions create a sphere different than riding lessons. In lessons, we use exercises to create a "sense" of being competitive and often simulate competitions as part of the preparations for competing. These are *teaching aids* for learning better riding skills; whether a student competes or not. But real life competitions, even local ones, are different. Competing is striving to do one's best (on a given day) measured against the same efforts by the other entrants. Generally, one winner emerges, with a number of "runner ups." Equestrian competitions usually feature: basic rules available beforehand; skills tested individually or in groups; and an impartial judge or judges whom are applying judging standards according to objective or subjective directives. Interestingly, most disciplines of the equestrian sports have rather stiff rules concerning coaching during competitions often resulting in competitor elimination if violated. Therefore, "coaching" generally occurs during preparations, warm ups and following competing when feedback is given to the competitor regarding their quality of performance. Lets look at helpful strategies for coaching *at* equestrian competitions.

ORGANIZING YOUR OVERALL APPROACH TO COACHING - BEFOREHAND - WILL ENABLE YOUR COMPETITOR TO DO THEIR BEST ON THAT GIVEN DAY. Typically, when coaches provide step by step coaching prior to competing, especially during the warm-up, a softer review of competition performance results. Conversely, when coaches leave the preparations and control of the warm-up to the competitor, more critical reviews are in store. While individual coaching styles might lean toward one of these approaches more than the other; all coaches should be capable of facilitating *either* approach. Be sure your competitor knows - beforehand - what your coaching plan is for that given competition and why. This allows your student to organize *their* planning for competing and helps to ease competition anxiety. Amidst the numerous rules that can be forgotten at the spur of the moment, unforeseen things that can occur, tension which interferes with performance and so on......... solid planning *with your student* prior to the competition is most ideal.

EFFECTIVE COACHING TOOLS AT THE COMPETITION INCLUDE: quick quizzes or reviews of relevant rules or patterns *just* prior to performance; encouraging teamwork between peers preparing to compete (leave the "competing" for the ring); applying competitive strategies such as directing a warm up to include *certain* drills to sharpen performance; advise on competitive strategies for "in the ring"; suggest relaxation techniques to decrease nervous tension such as deep breathing for the rider or a long walk for the horse; manage time, to help "peak" performance in the ring rather than the warm-up area; encouraging positive mental rehearsals of their forth coming performance; spot checks of tack, dress, required equipment, etc.

INDIVIDUALIZE YOUR COACHING AS MUCH AS POSSIBLE. Successfully choosing *what* degree of support and *what* degree of push is needed for *each* student-competitor is the mark of an experienced coach who individualizes their coaching. Naturally, larger numbers of students being coached on a given day and/or if the coach is a competitor as well (which is often the case in equestrian sports), results in less individual attention available compared to a coach who has only one or two competitors and is not competing themselves. However, individual attention, is not necessarily *individualizing* coaching. Individualizing coaching is taking important principles and making them relevant to *that* competitor's needs *at an exact time of benefit*. For example "Susie, do not practice any more flying changes before your reining pattern - stick to exercises at the jog until you go into the ring" and in the next breath this coach says to Danny: "practice a few more changes to the left.... I think they can improve." Naturally, competitors who receive considerable individual attention, *individualized* to their competitive needs will be hard to beat! Good Luck!

TIPS FOR TEACHING ONCE A WEEK RIDERS:

The instructional challenge for teaching once a week riders, is the reduced *speed* with which these riders progress. A large population of leisure riders can only swing enough time or finances to ride once a week. Unfortunately, riding once a week limits fitness *for* riding and hampers the muscle memory achieved by regular riding. Each week, a considerable amount of ride time is spent re-establishing muscle memory rather than using muscle memory. These riders are more subject to being stiff and sore following *each* weekly ride. While cross training through participation in other sports and exercise programs will help the once a week rider with *general* fitness, it is riding horses that builds riding stamina and riding skills. Furthermore, foggy memories with respect to terms, definitions, (etc.) is all too common due to limited "use" during once a week participation. Hands down, equestrians who ride three times a week or more *are* advantaged for *learning* horseback riding skills. Meanwhile, the once a week rider is usually a *very* dedicated enthusiast. They often study horseback riding more diligently than those who ride frequently. Their passion for horses helps to compensate for their limited involvement. Aside from being sure our progression of lessons take into account these challenging aspects common to once a week riding, we can best serve these riders by encouraging a minimum "general fitness" program between lessons, and by creating ways to "take home" some aspect of their riding. Here are two example strategies for "taking home" riding.

BETWEEN LESSONS, ENCOURAGE YOUR STUDENTS TO MENTALLY PRACTICE THE *SPECIFIC RIDING SKILLS* THEY ARE IN THE PROCESS OF IMPROVING. While once a week riders are often diligent about "mentally practicing" riding skills, be sure they are diligently practicing skills related to *their* level of riding. The mental practice most helpful to improve riding skills, is the mental practice of those skills in the midst of being improved or attempted for the first time. This means visualizing themselves with better balance at the canter; not pulling back on the reins as the horse begins a western spin; being able to stand in stirrups *elasticity* while the horse negotiates varied terrain; etc. While competitive sports researchers have proven that positive mental practice of specific skills helps to provide an edge in skill development for elite athletes, the mental practice of skills well beyond one's present abilities classifies as day dreaming. While day dreaming certainly holds merit for goal setting and motivation, this practice does little to bolster muscle "memory." Mental practice is most famous for the gains achieved in terms of muscle memory and the mental organization of sub-skills needed to successfully achieve a new skill.

ONCE A WEEK RIDERS BENEFIT FROM PERIODIC "TAKE HOME" VIDEOS, PICTURES AND TEXT. While it is hard to justify but a small portion of *any* once a week rider's *lesson time* on watching a video, analyzing pictures much less reading an article, *taking home* these educational tools can help to solve this dilemma. Videos can be of their personal riding, of others, or a professionally made video from your personal library you feel it is timely they watch. Text could be your favorite book on riding of which they are to read a particular chapter of, or a relevant article you have copied and provided to them. The key to utilizing take home images and text is careful selection on the instructor's part. These take home tools need to be manageable and useful to the student and instructor alike. Two examples are:

Example #1: instead of a parent taping the *entire* riding lesson, ask them to only tape the *last* exercise. Close your lesson with the instructions to review, at home, this footage and come to the next lesson prepared to self-critique their last exercise with respect to x, y & z. Example #2: using old magazines, select and cut out, four pictures (no captions) of horses and riders displaying a particular fault you see your rider struggling with. Also select one "good example" picture. Randomly number these pictures. Put them in an envelope. At the end of an appropriate lesson, give this envelope to your student -

homework. They are to analyze and rate the pictures. At the next lesson they are to return the envelope marked with their answers. Evaluation of their answers will be provided during that lesson or the next. Meanwhile, you have the pictures back to use again, plus you can file your student's answers for future reference or use.

For the once a week rider, " *take home* " exercises are in a sense, " *take home riding*"; have fun creating these exercises!

Chapter Seven

TEACHING TOOLS & TECHNIQUES

TIPS TO CREATE CHALKBOARDS IN YOUR RING:

L ots of devices can serve as a chalkboard in a riding ring - instructors are well known for using their heel or a whip in the sand of a ring to create an instant chalkboard. But aside from the "impromptu" chalkboards, it is wonderful to have a real life chalkboard available on ring side, not just in your tack room for the rainy day lessons. Quick erase boards seem to work just as well. Now lets look at what an actual or impromptu chalkboard can do for us in teaching riding.

CHALKBOARDS ARE GREAT FOR: LISTING GOALS, IMPORTANT POINTS OR KEY ITEMS TO ACCOMPLISH THAT DAY. A chalkboard used within the lesson can help highlight key points for a student to keep track of during the lesson. For example: a group lesson is working on keeping their circles round. You have discussed and listed four priorities for these riders, in order of importance. "Class - most important to keeping your circles getting rounder is *looking* around the circle while you are on it - look forward to each quarter point while on your circles; *eyes are listed #1 on the board.* Secondly, to improve a circle shape, check your lateral balance; fix your balance errors first; *check your lateral balance is listed #2 on the board.* And last, improve your horse's track on the circle with the proper leg correction first, *then* the proper rein correction next; *leg correction is listed #3 and rein correction is listed #4.*" Now they begin their practice. You have instructed your students to trot five circles or so, then walk once around the ring to rest, then trot five circles, and so on. During the rests at walk, your students have been encouraged to review the board for the priorities of the lesson, plus watch their classmates practice.

During their practice, you have been critiquing one student at a time for some individual attention. Now it is time for a longer rest and back to the chalkboard to collect the group. "Harry:

- review for us your last circle with respect to these 4 priorities"..... and so on goes your review with the assistance of the chalkboard.

CHALKBOARDS ALSO ALLOW US TO CREATE A PICTURE OR A LIST TOGETHER WITH OUR STUDENTS. Effective teaching is not merely providing information, providing a list or providing a picture. Sound teaching techniques also include guiding and encouraging students to be creative themselves. Thus, they are *applying* what they have learned which results in more "answers" being discovered. For example: it is time for a particular class to attempt a little harder course of 8 fences over a particular arrangement of jumps. They have just finished jumping an uncomplicated course over these jumps. During a 5 minute rest, at the ring chalkboard, you ask these students to help you design a harder course to jump next. Fence by fence they design a more difficult course with your assistance. This is done with *white* chalk. Then you go back with *blue* chalk and overlay the track of the easier course they did earlier to compare the difference. This highlights the increased difficulty that has been created. Now they are prepared to give their creation a try.

PICTURES MADE ON THE CHALKBOARD TEND TO BE MORE EXACT THAN VERBAL DIALOGUE IN PROVIDING FEEDBACK TO A STUDENT ABOUT SPECIFICS OF RIDING POSITION AND PERFORMANCE PATTERNS. When instructors say to..... "Susie - you need to put your shoulders more in front of your hips going up the hill" .....we are only touching the tip of the iceberg. How much in front of her hips? How does this relate to the horse's physic and balance? To answer these questions and others, a lot more dialogue would be needed. Furthermore, when the student tries again.....we may discover we failed to paint the proper picture in the student's head with words. Whereas, chalkboards allow us to draw an actual picture to our liking. Pictures are more exact, answer many questions at one time and save your vocal cords. Perhaps this is where the saying "a picture is worth a thousand words" came from!

TIPS FOR CREATING TEACHING APPLIANCES:

Teaching appliances help to *bridge* learning gaps. Popular and well known teaching appliances for horseback riding include: *a neck strap* - usually an english stirrup leather wrapped around the horse's neck, available for a rider to grab with one or both hands rather than balancing on the horse's mouth through the reins; *stirrup ties* - twine running through the inside of the stirrup and around the girth to steady the rider's leg position, stirrup ties <u>should</u> be used with safety stirrups; *a whip behind the rider's back and through their elbows*

- used to improve posture and/or to achieve a bend in the rider's elbows. Teaching appliances can save the day for learning plateaus. Teaching appliances can also increase safety for the student. For riding instruction, lets define teaching appliances to be those gadgets or pieces of rider equipment which instructors use to temporarily constrain or guide students during their learning. The result is a new feel, an improved position and/or an increased skill. Similar to horse training gadgets, these teaching appliances are rider training gadgets.

THE CHOICE TO USE A TEACHING APPLIANCE SHOULD ALWAYS BE WEIGHED AGAINST THE RISK OF DEVELOPING STUDENT DEPENDENCY ON THAT APPLIANCE. A common example of this is the popular use of chaps in english and western riding to quickly stabilize the rider's seat and legs. Chaps provide "stick to" power. Chaps can be a *wonderful* support for a capable rider who is out of shape but needs security while riding a greener horse. Chances are, this rider will get fit quickly and could easily discard their chaps in a short period of time. However, chaps are all too often loved by another type student. This student is hooked on the additional security chaps can and do provide. Usually, this scenario begins with the instructor recommending chaps as a means to gain a *new feel* for a more secure seat. "Wow" exclaims Susie, " this is what you mean by sit tighter!" With the *assistance* of the chaps, Susie achieves the better seat. Naturally, Susie likes riding in the chaps and over time she will be at high risk for becoming hooked on the chaps. Every instructor who suggests that a student ride with a teaching appliance (chaps in this case), must also be accountable for guiding the student away from becoming dependent *on* the appliance. In Susie's case, periodically asking Susie to remove her chaps will help her achieve this. Susie should be striving to ride as well without the chaps as with the chaps.

ASIDE FROM USING THOSE *TEACHING APPLIANCES* YOU ARE FAMILIAR WITH, ALLOW NECESSITY, TO BE THE MOTHER OF TEACHING APPLIANCE INVENTION. Be creative! Amanda, has flexible ankles. But following month after month of instruction, she *still* cannot coordinate getting her heels *down*. Out of desperation, you decide to strap some jogging weights onto Amanda's heels. Meanwhile, you explain to Amanda that you will continue to work on other things during the next few lessons and address the weights on her heels several lessons down the road. After a few rides, Amanda's body begins to take the path of least resistance. Her heels start to drop! After a few more lessons, you decide to try taking the weights off to see if she can begin to coordinate pushing her heels down herself. Yes she can! Furthermore, Amanda describes that because of the weights on her heels, she now has a clearer sense of where her heels *are* in relation to her stirrups. Even if she forgets at times to sink her heels down, this new measure she can now sense, her heels in relation to her stirrups, helps her to determine *how* drawn up her heels are. Success!

SOME OTHER CREATIVE TEACHING APPLIANCES INCLUDE: *The use of baling twine for reins* - useful for heavy handed riders (their hands will get sore if they pull too much); *using colored marked reins* - helps riders stay at the same place on the reins; *a hand hold strap* (this is a strap that connects to the D rings of an english saddle) - enables a rider to secure their seat from the pommel area; ...... and the list of teaching appliances can hopefully go on and on!

TIPS ON USING VIDEO TAPING IN YOUR LESSONS:

The opportunity for students to see themselves "in action" provides numerous learning advantages. In the past, still pictures (through an artist or camera) have provided riders a glimpse of their skills, posture and balance. Current day riders have a great advantage. They *also* have easy access to high quality video taping with sound. Lets look at the various ways we can incorporate this wonderful tool into our riding lessons.

NATURALLY, THE FIRST STEP IS TO GET FOOTAGE OF YOUR STUDENTS FOR LESSON PURPOSES. Once you announce your intentions, most riders are happy to be video taped. The next step of course is, *reviewing* the video footage. This also needs to be a part of your lesson. Here are some ideas for filming and reviewing video footage:

As part of your riding evaluation for new students, or during the beginning of a riding lesson semester, structure one of your lessons to be half mounted and half unmounted. Video tape your student's ride, then review it with them in your office. Keep this footage on file. Use it later as a document of progress. It is very motivational for any student to see how much progress they have made over a period of time.

Try taping your students at a distance, during their practice of an exercise. While filming, provide them verbal feedback about their practice into the microphone. Be sure you are far enough away, that they cannot hear your comments while they are practicing. This allows them to concentrate on their performance without being "coached" through it. At the end of their practice, send them home with the video tape which also contains your comments to review as homework. This will delay your feedback until they have the visual "re-run" of their performance to watch together with your comments. Follow up at the beginning of your next lesson; reactions and questions may be plentiful!

Tape your students doing a particular exercise that needs improvement. Have a TV and video machine set up on ring side. Show your students the footage of their practice during their rest break of the lesson. Be sure to provide them information on *what* they need to improve and *how.* Tape their next practice. Back to the TV to watch and compare their first practice with the second; and so on. Don't be surprised if the equines are just as interested in watching the video as the humans.

For reviewing and evaluating position and mechanics, still pause, frame advance and slow motion replay are extremely useful. Proper swing of the rider's hips, the rider aids and their timing in relation to the horse's movements, and a rider's hand position during the moment of a canter depart are just a few skills that can be more accurately seen and evaluated with the assistance of slow motion replay. Instructors can help students see mechanical and form problems and their relationship to the horse's movements with the assistance of these video features.

Use the focus feature on your video to emphasize details of position. Zero in on a straighter back or a seat that no longer bounces - *yea!* Zero in on hands that are unsteady or legs that are swinging - *boo!* The focus feature will enable you to *focus* your student's review. With younger children and some adults this will be a particular advantage in directing them to observe the details in question.

CONSIDER DEVELOPING A VIDEO LIBRARY IN YOUR BARN. Like those familiar book shelves in most barns today, video libraries are also great. Aside from commercially produced videos, the videos you take of your lessons can be useful when cataloged by the topic of the lesson. For example: learning how to mount, learning about leads, learning how to sit the trot "101", and so on. You might even want to get fancy and cross reference topics and students. Endless possibilities!

TIPS ON USING ANALOGIES EFFECTIVELY:

For teaching, analogies are a *powerful* tool. Analogies convey comparisons that help create a desired mental image or refer to a particular feeling or sensation. Furthermore, analogies are fun! For an instructor, analogies are rather like a tick, tack, toe game. The process goes a bit like this. A proper comparison is selected. The instructor then links it to the lesson at hand. The analogy provides a connection for the student .... and bingo, the lesson or a part thereof, is achieved by the student. This is a popular technique because instructors enjoy relating skills to other skills. It is an effective teaching tool because analogies allow instructors *and* students to personalize a particular riding skill. Lets look at effective ways to use the tick, tack, toe analogy tool.

WHEN SELECTING A PROPER ANALOGY, THE COMPARISON SHOULD BE *FAMILIAR* TO THE STUDENT. Now imagine you have a beginner group lesson of five students and you are using the analogy that proper steering of a horse is similar to how we steer a bike: inside hand back and outside hand goes forward. You delve into using this analogy with great enthusiasm and sincerity only to discover that two of these five adult beginners have never ridden a bike! After discovering this fauxpas, you do some fancy footwork and turn this "ooops" into homework: "well then George and Sarah, I guess you better go home and have your children or a friend teach you how to ride their bike!" Naturally it is best to choose your analogies based on daily skills, sport skills or riding skills that the students are *familiar* with. Since an analogy helps to shed light on the unknown, it is essential that your students can *relate to* the analogies you choose to use. Meanwhile, for the students who *have* ridden a bike, this analogy immediately provides sensory information to these students. They will know what to do with the reins for steering, what their arm movements will be and how the horse should turn - the same as turning a bike. Analogies can save a lot of teacher talk and let the students get on with practicing.

LINKING YOUR ANALOGY TO THE RIDING SKILL WILL BE MOST EFFECTIVE IF THE ANALOGY IS *STRONGLY SIMILAR* TO THE RIDING SKILL YOU ARE WORKING ON. Using analogies that require you to clarify various aspects or details are more tedious. Most effective are those analogies that will stand on their own. For example: Try to sit light as a feather. Flap your elbows like wings. Treat the reins like two sponges and try squeezing the water out of the sponges (reins). Pretend your horse is no wider than a balance beam. Try to sit in the middle of that balance beam while your horse is turning. Close your legs around the horse in a firm hand shake fashion from hip to ankle. Proper position in riding is the same as a ballerina's: stretched but graceful. Try to look like a ballerina. A rider's hips should feel weightless in the two-point position, like a balloon floating upward. These are some examples of analogies that are strongly similar to the riding skills being worked on. They stand on their own.

AN ANALOGY GIVEN BY THE INSTRUCTOR PROVIDES A CONNECTION *FOR* THE STUDENT IN LEARNING THE LESSON; BUT AT TIMES, STUDENTS WILL PROVIDE *US* ANALOGIES OF THEIR OWN. Frequently when you ask students to put a concept or description in their own words or describe how something felt, student analogies will come forth. These student produced analogies give us feedback about our student's learning. They are much more valuable in assessing learning than yes/no answers to questions. Encourage student produced analogies when you can. Student produced analogies, solicited or not, will help the student to personalize the skill to their riding. Furthermore, student produced analogies can be handy to catalog for future use - they are often original and will add to your analogy grab bag.

Chapter Eight

STUDENT SKILLS

TIPS FOR WARMING UP A RIDER, PHYSICALLY:

While outdoor temperature has a bearing on the comfort and ease for riders during a warm up, this subject is devoted to the *internal* physiological warming up riders should achieve to reach optimal performance and reduce sports injuries. Effective *internal* physiological warm up can only be achieved by the *rider's* energies.

PROPERLY WARMING UP A RIDER MEANS RIDING MOVEMENTS PERFORMED IN MODERATION FOR THE RESPECTIVE LEVEL OF THE STUDENT. Another words, instructors should choose exercises which ask for *moderate duration*, *moderate range of movement* and *moderate exertion* during a warm up period. Warm-up exercises lay the foundation on which intense physical exercise can safely be done. Furthermore, the proper warm-up of a rider will enable a student to achieve their individual maximum athletic performance during any given ride. Inadequate warm ups, result in less than normal skill performance. The warm up period should lead smoothly into the intensity portion of a lesson followed by a cool down. A warm up that is "too much too fast" contributes to sports injuries and a warm up that is "too little to be prepared" results in less athletic achievement. An ideal warm-up will enable the rider to transition *without a leap* from the warm-up exercises to the intense work of the day. Naturally, the exercises chosen for novice students will be vastly different from those for advanced students. As riders advance in skill development, *learned* skills become automatic or naturalized. Thus, these learned skills become the foundation of future warm ups while that same skill would have been the intensity portion during previous riding. Since horseback riders are of numerous of body types mounted on numerous equine body types this produces an infinite number of conditions for which *specific* warming up strategies may be needed. For example, a short legged rider with tight groin hamstrings will undoubtedly benefit from more time to stretch out at the walk when mounted on a broad-backed Clydesdale cross than needed when mounted on a slapsided Akhal-Teke or Thoroughbred . Generally, warming up a rider properly is the opportunity to prepare the rider's body with moderate stretching, suppling, strengthening, balancing and/or coordinating - as needed for the lesson - *prior* to the use of these skills to a *problem*.

UNLIKE OTHER SPORTS, JUST THE SHEER MOTION OF THE HORSE CREATES MOVEMENT IN THE HUMAN BODY. For therapeutic riding, this horse created movement is an essential aspect of why horseback riding is successfully used *for* therapy. Perhaps it is also due to this component, that *able* bodied riders seem to enjoy an edge over other sports in the department of warming up. Take the extreme example of a tightly muscled rider. This rider has short ligament attachments in their joints and a high proportion of slow twitch fibers to their muscles. As long as this rider is relaxed mentally (about riding), the physiological progression to stretching out this rider's tight body, particularly their trunk, occurs rather quickly due to the movement and warmth of the *horse's* body combined with theirs. There seems to exist a synergistic element to the combination of horses and riders warming up together. However, in the case of a nervous or a *very* novice rider, "floor" warm-up exercises *just prior* to mounting are desirable and beneficial for physical and emotional safety.

FOR DETERMINING THE PROPER WARM-UP EXERCISES OF THE DAY, AN INSTRUCTOR SHOULD PLAN BACKWARDS FROM THE INTENSE PORTION OF THAT LESSON. For example, the next lesson an intermediate group of jumping riders will have, is to practice over a small course of two foot fences without stirrups. Physiologically, riding over fences without stirrups takes strength. The rider has to be able to keep the short stirrup leg (minus the aid of the stirrups) plus the two-point position, without pinching, in order to be successful. Pinching one's legs while jumping creates many losses of balance. Thus, the warm up of this lesson needs to focus on the student's leg muscles, though not encouraging gripping or pinching. Therefore, frequent transitions from the halt to walk to trot to walk or halt are chosen. First with stirrups, then for a brief time without stirrups prior to jumping. Once jumping, initially the student starts with their stirrups then progresses to the intense portion of this lesson, small jumps *without* stirrups.

TIPS FOR COOLING DOWN A RIDER, PHYSICALLY:

In our last topic, the example rider progressed to jumping small jumps without stirrups, generally a taxing experience. This topic is devoted to the subject of cooling the *rider* down physically, from the exertion of a reasonable, though sometimes taxing, lesson plan.

PARTICULARLY WHEN *ANAEROBIC* WORK HAS BEEN DONE, CARE MUST BE TAKEN TO *COOL DOWN SLOWLY* TO LESSEN THE EFFECTS OF LACTIC ACID BUILD UP IN MUSCLES. Anaerobic work is intense exercise which is done without oxygen supply to the muscles. We are in anaerobic exercise, when the load of physical exertion makes us run out of breath and in short order, run out of steam too. During anaerobic exercise, lactic acid is produced. If severe, this lactic acid will cramp a rider *during* exercise, grinding them to a halt. If not severe, most riders simply have sore muscles the next day. To cool down a rider who has reached their anaerobic threshold, first allow this rider to catch their breath for a few minutes. Then, return to aerobic work for at least five minutes and better yet, ten minutes. Aerobic exercise is a level of exertion where the rider can comfortably carry on a conversation. The aerobic exercise *following* anaerobic exercise defuses the lactic acid build up in a rider's muscles. The result: *far less sore and tight muscles the next day.* Conversely, if the horse needs to conclude their exercise for that day, have the rider dismount, walk the horse out on foot (certainly a brisk walk is aerobic), then finish with appropriate floor exercises for the muscles taxed.

WHILE HEART RATES ARE THE SCIENTIFIC WAY TO CALCULATE THE DIFFERENCE BETWEEN AEROBIC AND ANAEROBIC EXERCISE, *PERCEIVED* EXERTION IS JUST ABOUT AS ACCURATE, QUICKER AND EASIER. To assess exertion during exercise, ask your rider how hard they are working. Give them a minimum of five choices. For example: *1) not hard 2) somewhat hard 3) hard 4) very hard 5) extremely hard.* These translate into: *1) not hard = below aerobic 2) somewhat hard = aerobic 3) hard = aerobic though close to anaerobic 4) very hard = anaerobic 5) extremely hard = anaerobic.* As a rider gets fitter, more strenuous exercise will be needed to reach the aerobic and anaerobic thresholds. Another valuable indicator of fitness is a rider's recovery rate. The more fit a rider is, the faster their recovery to normal breathing and a resting heart rate following strenuous exercise.

FOR *NEW* MUSCLES USED IN A PARTICULAR LESSON, STRETCHING AT THE *END* OF THE LESSON IS BENEFICIAL. Examples of more strenuous lessons which create this scenario are: raising or lowering stirrup length several holes; going from a horse who does not "pull" to one who does; switching from a short strided smooth moving horse to a long strided, bounding horse; posting to the trot for the first time instead of sitting *or* sitting to the trot for the first time instead of posting; riding without *one* stirrup; elevating one's arm position to ride saddleseat instead of hunt seat, and so on. When new muscles are being used during a lesson, generally the student is aware of the difference. Frequently students will comment they are using muscles they never knew they had! Rarely is this painful. Usually the use of new muscles just feels "different." Take care though, newly found muscles *tire* quickly. Excessive exercise of newly found muscles *will be* painful and the cost can be a serious injury. A useful guideline is: once new muscles tire, rest. One more *brief* repetition of exercise using these new muscles can be comfortably accomplished following a *generous* rest. Numerous repetitions, even with rest between, is risky. Instead, wait for another day. Muscle *endurance* is built over time. For cooling down a rider who has exerted new muscles, stretching will help to sooth newly exerted muscles and counter the involuntary contraction that can accompany the exertion of a new found muscle group. *"Stretching"* is simply using the counterpart muscles from those exerted. For our saddleseat rider example, this would be spending a few minutes having the rider dangle their arms at their sides and then stretching their fingertips toward the ground. Be willing to do some research for choosing or creating exercises that will *indeed*, provide meaningful stretching. Physical therapists and related references will be your best resource. Apply your findings carefully and request student feedback at your *next* lesson.

TIPS FOR IMPROVING BALANCE:

Many aspects of developing a rider's balance are similar to improving a rider's coordination. Sports researchers confirm that balancing and coordinating are quite *unique* to each sport and are best developed by *doing* that sport. Therefore, practice time in the saddle is fundamental. Developing solid balancing skills at *all* levels bolsters confidence, keeps your students in the saddle and makes equestrian activities comfortable for the horse as well. Here are three important principles to incorporate in your lesson planning for improving riders' balance.

FIRST, BE SURE TO INSTALL "SAFETY NETS" WHEN WORKING ON BALANCING SKILLS. Because an "off balance" rider can be in jeopardy of falling and/or loosing their nerve, installing *safety nets* is similar to a "spotter" in gymnastics. Some examples of safety nets in riding instruction are: a school master horse who will stop or step under a falling rider; a neck strap to grab if the student's balance gets really off; permission to walk or stop to re-organize balance in case of an emergency; soft footing in case a rider might fall; a voice trained horse to allow the instructor to assist; chaps/saddle tight/leather seated breeches for extra stability on a challenging mount; tools a student can use for reorganizing *without* stopping - such as changing from sitting to posting trot during an extended trot if balance has been lost. Proper safety nets are as essential for advanced students as beginner students.

SECONDLY, BE SURE TO ISOLATE A MANAGEABLE STEP OF BALANCING TO IMPROVE FOR EACH STUDENT. If you cannot come up with an appropriate safety net, then chances are you have *surpassed* what is a manageable step for that student. Obviously, smaller steps are better than giant leaps but remain open to a student's desire to challenge themselves. If your student has mustarded up the courage to try a particular skill and you have an appropriate safety net in place, why not? Naturally the flip side of that coin is the overly confident student. These students will try *anything*. They need our help in putting "caution" into the equation. Choosing a manageable step does not mean the student has to master that step that day. But it *should mean*, they will be able to make *forward progress* and master that step in the near future. Until a balancing skill is mastered, it usually does not feel all that great. For some students this chaos can be hard. It is rough, unstable, and in extreme cases the student is even asking themselves "why am I doing this? I do not seem to have the talent!" Be prepared to do some hand holding for the bigger steps of balancing skills you are seeking to help your student with. It is the rare student who does not need or benefit from your emotional support. Choosing smaller steps allows you to groom confidence and joy. Choosing bigger steps over and over will burnout even the gutsiest student.

LAST, GIVE YOUR STUDENTS TOOLS TO HELP THEM MEASURE THEIR OWN IMPROVEMENT OF BALANCING. The most natural tool we do not have to teach students about, but we need to *remind them to use*, is their sense of *feel*. Riding in better balance with the horse *feels better* even though at times this is harder or easier work. When a rider is having to work harder *physically* to achieve this better balanced feeling, it is most helpful to remind them that this state of harmony and equilibrium is being achieved because of what they are *doing*. Likewise, when a rider needs to work less hard to achieve better balance, it is often a revelation that *doing less* is in fact desirable. Mechanical tools of measurement will also help your students assess their own progress. Is the student's chest in line with the middle of the horse's mane during that circle they are working on? Can the student see their shoulders over their hips, in a mirror or using the shadows provided by the sun? Sharing "feel" as well as "mechanical" evaluation tools with your students will help them assess their own skills during lessons *and* during non-lesson rides.

TIPS TO HELP YOUR RIDERS DEVELOP THEIR COORDINATION

To coordinate a particular riding skill, muscling, balance and timing are required. Sports researchers confirm that balancing and coordinating are quite unique to each sport. Therefore, coordination skills are best developed for a sport by *doing* the sport. Whereas body strength and flexibility can be developed in a multitude of ways. Lets look at how we can direct student practice to cultivate and refine coordination skills.

FIRST, ENCOURAGE YOUR STUDENTS TO PRACTICE THE SKILL THEY ARE LEARNING TO COORDINATE, UNTIL THEY TIRE. This is because more exact timing tends to evolve with continuous practice. Thus if a rider practices only a little, does something else, then returns to practice a little more, they are starting up their "timing" with each short practice. Little ground is gained. Whereas, providing for a lengthier practice session, enables the student to refine their timing and habituate the desired skills. With continuous practice, a rider develops muscle reflexes which make the coordination of new skills easier and easier to achieve. More ground is gained. When the student tires, rest and repeat, or go onto another task for that day.

Put yourself in a ring setting. Your student is working on sitting the trot properly while they primarily influence the horse with their legs for steering. You have directed your rider to make three circles down each long side of the ring. This provides the student repetitive transitions from a straight line to a curved line to practice steering with their legs. Occasionally the rider is instructed to change the rein on the diagonal and continue the exercise in the other direction so both sides of the horse and rider get a workout. Initially, the rider has a hard time balancing on the first couple of circles and forgets to use their legs to steer. Then, the next circle goes much better, and the next circle is beautiful but the rider is late to transition their legs from the bending position to riding for a straight line, so the horse weaves onto the straight line. So on and so forth it goes. But circle after circle, the number of correctly ridden circles increases. Practicing over a longer period of time creates a "roll." Naturally, as the student tires this "roll" fades. It is time to rest, go onto something else or call it a day.

FOR COORDINATING A NEW SKILL, DETERMINE IF YOUR STUDENT WILL BEST BENEFIT PRINCIPALLY FROM AUDITORY, VISUAL OR KINESTHETIC INSTRUCTION PROVIDED BY THE INSTRUCTOR. Auditory instruction is talking the student through the skill. Visual instruction is giving the student a demonstrator to watch or follow and imitate. Kinesthetic instruction is having the student use the sensations of the exercise to guide their practice. For visual and kinesthetic instruction there is less instructor talk during practice. When using these two methods, instructors principally provide verbal feedback following student practice. Your decision to use auditory, visual or kinesthetic instruction should be based on which method you feel works best for guiding the riding skill at hand, together with, what method works best with the particular students you are teaching. For example: "up/down" or "one/two" are popular verbal instructions used to help new riders coordinate posting to the trot. Rightly so - these are proven verbal instructions that work. But for a student who learns easier from visual instructions, you might want to saddle up a horse, ride next to your student, get your horses trotting side by side and provide a visual up/down example for your student to copy. Meanwhile, other students have a keen sense for movement. Before practice begins provide this student the sensory information they need. They should sit when they feel a sink and stand when they feel a rise to the horse's gait. Then as they practice, the *horse's* trot does the rest.

TIPS TO ACHIEVE RIDER RELAXATION:

Rider relaxation can be most easily split into two categories: physical relaxation and mental relaxation. At times riders can sense their tensions while at other times they cannot. Whether an instructor is dealing with physical or mental tension, or both, your first effort should be to determine if the student is *aware* of their tension. At times simple observation will provide you the answer, while discussions prove fruitless. Yet in other circumstances, discussion with your student will be the *only* aspect that will provide you the true answer, because what you *see* would lead you astray. To further complicate things, there are times in the "learning curve" where it is *unrealistic* to expect our students to *be able to* relax. Nerves during a first ride in an open field or a tighter upper body that results when a rider works on strengthening their legs are two common examples of this. Now, let us study situations where it *is* realistic for our students to achieve relaxation but they are not relaxed - *yet.*

IF YOU DETERMINE YOUR STUDENT IS UNAWARE OF THEIR TENSION, DECIDE IF IT IS BENEFICIAL FOR THEM TO *BE* AWARE. With some tensions, particularly those that do not involve fear or clashing values, awareness will help the student to work through their tension. In these cases the student needs to *experience* their lack of relaxation in a fashion they can perceive. This is where teaching is not "telling", but instead, directing the student's "experiencing." Teaching techniques which are most helpful for this are: have your student do an exercise as tense as possible (careful with safety here), then as relaxed as possible. This asks a student to relax the "tense" state they created. They gain both something to compare and a sense for "releasing" their tense state. Using teaching props or exercises that, in a sense, trigger relaxation are also valuable. For example, getting a student to breath with deep regular breaths while doing a jumping course induces physical relaxation and even seems to relax the mind. Popular with horseback riding instructors and certainly a valid strategy is to identify the tension present in the student *while* practice is in progress.

CONVERSELY, IN OTHER CASES IT WILL BE MOST DESIRABLE TO WORK ON A STUDENT'S TENSION MUCH LIKE HOW THE TOOTH FAIRY OPERATES. Physical and mental relaxation, improves our abilities to be skillful. There are those wonderful times in teaching riding, when our students wake up and find their tensions gone. But much like the tooth fairy, the instructor has been hard at work for perhaps even months, in subtle ways, nursing along this transition. The reward for the child beyond the prize under the pillow the next morning, will be the new mature tooth to follow. Likewise, the reward for "released" tensions in riding, is our ability to be in better harmony with our horses. This result, all riders can detect and appreciate. Operating behind the scenes like the tooth fairy, is most desirable where fear, clashing values or gross skill deficits are concerned. A tooth fairy instructor incorporates exercises into the lesson that will *induce* relaxation through practice. Tooth fairies also avoid getting into battles with the student on principles. Above all, tooth fairies are infinitely patient because behind the scenes operations take *time.* For example, an intermediate level group of riders all stiffen their legs too much. During the next quarter of riding lessons you announce that each day they ride, you want them to spend several minutes of their warm up on dropping either stirrup, one at a time for several strides, then picking it back up. By the end of the next 3 month period they should strive to be able to drop either stirrup for several strides and pick it up, *smoothly,* in walk, trot *and* canter. While at face value, this is an exercise to build coordination skills; with time and practice it will *also* relax the rider's leg - the tooth fairy is at work!

TIPS TO HELP STUDENTS SENSE MOVEMENT AND RHYTHM

Of equal value in riding, is a rider's ability to feel their *own* movement and rhythm as well as that of the *horse's*. As we know, maximum harmony is achieved when a horse and rider move together as one - *in harmony*. As students progress, their abilities to sense their own movement and rhythm and that of the horse, should escalate at a relatively equal rate. Without this, mechanical or forced riding skills result. Sensing movement and rhythm is the initial phase of "feeling." Once a rider and horse have achieved perfected skills at a particular task, little to no conscious thought is needed to maintain the harmony - sensing has then become rather automatic. Lets look at that initial phase of "feeling" - the ability to sense movement and rhythm.

GENERALLY, LESS TEACHER "TALK" IS DESIRABLE FOR THOSE LESSONS WHERE WE ARE TRYING TO HELP OUR STUDENTS SENSE MOVEMENT AND RHYTHM. Sensing movement and rhythm increases when the rider is listening to *their body* or the *horse's*; not a dialogue from the teacher. A wonderful example of teaching with less teacher "talk" is using music for your students to ride to during a lesson. Try developing your own music selections as a teaching tool. Select music for the tempo, time and beat which you would like your riders to achieve in the gait/s you are striving to improve. Selecting specific music to help your students achieve a particular rhythm assists both the riders and the horses. Horses love to get in step with music too! Another lesson plan using less teacher talk which highlights movement and rhythm is to ask your students to, for example, ride a jumping course while wearing earplugs. This maximizes the sensations of jumping. Taking away one of our senses increases the sensitivity of the remaining senses. Another popular and effective strategy is to have your student ride with their eyes shut. Be sure the logistics of your lesson account for safety and then give your student a task to focus on. For example: you have a student who needs to improve the swing of their seat in order to sit better *with* their horse's big canter. First you have this student close their eyes at walk going down one long side of the ring to focus on the movement of their hips swinging back and forth. This gets them familiar with closing their eyes. Next, they apply closing their eyes in canter. During a rest break ask them to describe how their hips felt; *your* critique should follow their description. Interesting observations and discoveries can result at this point, do not put words in your student's mouth by putting your comments first. Using any exercise in your lesson plan that curtails or takes away a student's crutch such as riding with no hands, no stirrups or bareback riding are also very effective in highlighting movement and rhythm.

TO INCREASE YOUR STUDENT'S SENSE OF PHYSICAL MOVEMENT AND RHYTHM, COMFORT AND DISCOMFORT PLAY A HELPFUL

ROLE. A horse who has a bouncy trot can help a student identify the need to increase their hip movement to sit with a bouncy trot; yet a smoother gaited horse would be essential to enable that same student to focus on the footfall of the trot gait. Perfecting a student's sense of movement takes an uncluttered mind. Additionally, sensing a new riding skill, quickly and repeatedly, takes practice which often involves some trial and error. Generally, rider comfort produces a green light, whereas discomfort produces a yellow or red light. Particularly when red and yellow lights turn green, the rider experiences a sensory light bulb. For example: a rider who balances on their hands will interfere with the horse using their head and neck properly. The horse's gaits are more jilted and horse's back is tense. As a rider accomplishes balancing independent of their hands, their horse's movement will become softer and more relaxed, both horse and rider become more comfortable. Encouraging your students to recognize *their* increased comfort and the *horse's*, increases sensitivity to movement and rhythm in general. As riders recognize the horse's comfort and discomfort and how this integrates with their own, they have achieved a higher level measure stick of movement and rhythm.

TIPS FOR INCREASING RIDER BODY AWARENESS:

Essentially, rider body awareness is kinesthesia. Random House Dictionary defines kinesthesia as: "the sensation of movement or strain in muscles, tendons and joints" another words, a rider's muscle sense. Some riders have limited experience with understanding their body's movement for achieving athletic skills, while other riders have a keen sense of their body which enables them to achieve equestrian skills quite easily. There are times when riders get absorbed (mentally) in the *horse's* kinesthesia preventing them from noticing or attending *to* their own kinesthesia. These are a few of the circumstances which horseback riding instructors face. Let's look at this subject more closely.

FIND EXERCISES OR WORDS THAT WILL ENHANCE YOUR STUDENTS' ABILITIES TO *SENSE THEIR OWN* BODY MOVEMENT. While most exercise programs are devoted to the instructional "policing" of any excessive straining to reduce muscle, tendon and joint injuries, this as a preoccupation, can interfere with horseback riders developing their own body awareness while riding. There exists, to a greater or lesser extent, a definitive cause and effect relationship while riding horses. Horses voice their opinions through movement; their sensory challenge. Conversely, much to the surprise of some students, jumping for the first time does not feel like they imagined it to and trying to "sit still" on a lumbering horse actually takes muscles. While these surprises are rarely new to the instructor, achieving an environment that enables the student to "discover" specific elements of their movement while riding can be quite challenging. Furthermore, kinesthesia somewhat falls short for the subject of describing horseback riders' body awareness because once a rider discovers "new" body awarenesses, horses frequently like to present the need to *use* these new skills, even in complex ways. Another words, horses' lesson plans do not always match the instructors! Thus, structure the learning environment to be as simple as possible, plus provide to the student sufficient practice repetitions for sensory study.

EXAGGERATION OF SENSATIONS AND THE ABSENCE OF SENSATIONS ARE HELPFUL TEACHING TOOLS. Take for example a rider who needs to increase their sense of where their lower leg is resting on the horse. When asked where their leg rests, in relation to the horse's anatomy, they are incorrect. Several solutions to increase their body awareness would be: put them on a horse with a different conformation in hope that this difference will help them feel what you see; put them on a horse who will express a difference when they achieve the lower leg position you are seeking; seek a horse who will *not* cooperate until they achieve the lower leg position desired.

AT TIMES THE DEGREE OF CONCENTRATION A RIDER HAS, INTERFERES WITH THEIR ACHIEVING BODY AWARENESS. You observe certain elements, the horse does too, but the rider....... does not. Frequently after a student achieves certain skills, when asked by the instructor "and did you know your hands were quiet during that exercise?" the student responds with a blank expression or a reluctant ..... "no." While sometimes attributed to the student *using* their body awareness on a working level (little awareness necessary), more often, this is a product of: they were "talked through" the exercise by you or the horse.

THE NATURALIZATION OF A PHYSICAL SKILL MEANS COMPLETE FAMILIARITY, AND ALSO MEANS THAT LITTLE TO NO CONSCIOUS THOUGHT IS NECESSARY TO PERFORM THAT SKILL. Translated into our teaching/learning environment of horseback riding skills, students who are using their body awareness to either ride their horse or to solve a problem with their horse are displaying a high level of rider body awareness. After all, it is through our control of body with which we communicate to our horse and then the world beyond. While all our senses help in the strategy of riding, the rider's body movement is the resulting beautiful form of communication between horse and rider.

TIPS FOR INCREASING HORSE BODY AWARENESS:

This topic of teaching tips will focus on helping riders increase their awareness of the *horse's* locomotion. This subject is defined as: helping the rider improve their *perception* of the horse's locomotion and kinesthesia. While some riders possess a natural ability to sense the horse's body, other riders have to work diligently to achieve awareness of the horse's body *in motion*. The following teaching techniques will be helpful for increasing perception of equine kinesthesia. Most lesson plans can incorporate these ideas and in some cases, instructors might find it necessary to focus their lesson plan on this fundamental of horseback riding. Take care to apply these ideas with compassion for the horse.

ENCOURAGING EXAGGERATED MOTION FROM THE HORSE, CAN HELP A RIDER TO SENSE THEIR OWN LACK OF MOVEMENT. Particularly when a rider is compassionate and patient toward horses, an instructor will find it helpful to encourage a horse to exaggerate their locomotion. When riders feel out of control of the horse's motion, some individuals resist while others relax. For the riders who relax, exaggerated motion from the horse can be helpful with little danger. Utilizing the exaggerated motion of the horse for riders who resist, often results in more problems. With carefully planned limits, this strategy can be helpful for these tense riders, but the gamble is risky. Preferably, select other teaching strategies. For riders who can stay relaxed, here are several examples of instructor encouraged exaggerated motion of the horse: asking a horse to move a little faster with a cluck; using a "whoa" to aid the horse to slow down a bit more quickly; stepping toward a horse to move a horse laterally; asking a horse to come to the instructor; etc.

ENCOURAGE YOUR STUDENT TO UTILIZE THEIR *OTHER* SENSES TO AID THEM IN PERCEIVING THE HORSE'S LOCOMOTION. For example: students who find it difficult to feel the motion of the horse through their kinesthesia benefit from listening *for* the footfall of the horse's gaits. Additionally, as the student is ready, asking them to speak out loud the footfall they are hearing, enables the instructor to monitor the student's auditory incorporation of the horse's locomotion. While riding, utilizing eyesight for receiving visual movement information, frequently conquers a student's barrier to *perceiving* the horse's locomotion. Ways to aid a rider in receiving visual movement information are: riding in front of mirrors, looking at the reflections made on a pond, or watching shadows available at certain times of day. It would be rare for a student to be able to *concentrate on* and *correlate* several of their other senses simultaneously. Therefore, organize exercises that ask them to utilize *one* of their other senses at a time.

ENCOURAGE A RIDER TO MAKE SIMPLE MOVEMENTS AND ASSOCIATE THEM TO THE HORSE'S MOVEMENT. This helps a student feel the movements of the horse. Association of movement, provides contrasts which are sometimes comfortable and other times uncomfortable but most frequently, just plain new. For example: when a novice rider is encouraged to touch a particular part of the horse at a walk or faster, their movement is of assistance for the "discovery" of the horse's movement. Care should be taken on the instructor's part not to encourage excessive movement by the student which the horse may not tolerate. For some students, it will be more desirable to direct them to perform certain simple motions, then ask the student to correlate their motion to what was perceived from the horse.

INCREASED AWARENESS OF EQUINE KINESTHESIA IS AN EFFECTIVE TOOL FOR RIDERS TO ASSESS THEIR MOUNT'S EMOTIONS AND PHYSIOLOGICAL HEALTH. Particularly when a rider lacks patience or compassion for their mount, it is helpful to concentrate on improving awareness of their horse's kinesthesia. Unfortunately, some individuals lack interest on the subject of the horse's kinesthesia, locomotion and even at times, fitness too. Therefore, these students' particular needs will be best met through adjunct activities of the barn, horsemanship literature and role models.

TIPS FOR IMPROVING A RIDER'S SENSITIVITY TO PRESSURE:

Quite common in riding are student's misconceptions regarding sensitivity to pressure: personally and in principle. For humans, this problem can be further complicated by the horse's sensitivity pressure, of which, there are great variations based on breeding, rearing, formal training and age. On the one hand, we have students who do not want to "hurt" their horse. They tend to ride dangerously loose with not enough force to their aids to be assertive when necessary. On the other hand, we have riders who are unaware of the strength they are exerting on their horse. They sit stiffly, fixed and/or apply harsh aids due to poor balance or too much aggression. In many cases these misconceptions about proper sensitivities to pressure can lead to welfare problems for either the horse, the rider or both. Here are some teaching tools to try. If you get creative, variations of these teaching tools can unlock many doors for your students.

GENERALLY, IMPROVING A RIDER'S SENSITIVITY TO PRESSURE CAN BE BEST ACCOMPLISHED BY HELPING THE STUDENT TO GAIN THE PROPER *FEEL* OF THE DESIRED SENSATIONS. Here are several examples of *how* to accomplish just that. Example number one has been around for years; it still works: place *your* dollar bill (or more) under..... a rider's knee, thigh, seat or calf ...... choose where the student is loose and needs to tighten up. Naturally there is an incentive not to loose this money because the student gets to keep your contribution if it does not wind up on the ground. This game can be altered to as high a stakes as you can afford or to an amount you feel will motivate your student to "try" hard enough to discover *just* how much stronger they need to be. Be sure to remind this student that while they probably can afford to loose this money, they really cannot afford to miss out on developing a more secure seat. Example number two centers around the instructor gaining a feel for the exact pressure their student is applying then modulating the student's pressure to what is most appropriate. With the horse halted, hold both reins half way between your student's hands and the horse's bit. Now you are the horse's mouth. First ask your student to show you the contact *they* provide the horse (which you have been observing is too stiff and forceful). Next, reverse roles. Ask your student to be the *horse* to show you what feeling the horse gives them. Last, in *both* roles, *show* your student how they *should* feel to the horse and in turn, how the horse *will* feel to them. Example number three is well suited for conditions of a lesson where your student is continuing to ride: have your student begin riding. Ask them to pick, on a scale of 1-10 how straight they feel their posture is. This student selects 6 (they know you would not approve of anything higher because you are *always* correcting their slouch). Now it is your turn. Call out a number and *they* are to show you *that* posture. Use the whole scale if you like or select just a few numbers. If you ask them to demonstrate all 10 postures and they are able to accomplish this (even on a more or less basis) you will have helped them differentiate sensitive gradations of "bad" postures 0-4 and good postures 5-10. Quite an accomplishment!

AS STUDENTS PROGRESS, RE-DEFINING "GOOD RIDING" ON A SENSORY BASIS IS JUST AS NECESSARY AS THE NEED TO RE-DEFINE TERMINOLOGY. While a novice student will often need to "hang on" a bit more with their legs as a stepping stone to becoming "better" balanced - better balance eventually means very *little* hanging on with one's legs. Likewise, most beginning riders are discouraged from using the reins much at all, so they will not balance *on* the horse's mouth and will *learn* to use their legs. Meanwhile, the only way to accomplish advanced riding skills is to learn *how to use* the reins properly! For the student, this can seem like a Pandora's box on a sensory level let alone an emotional level. But if your students have been systematically progressed in their riding skills, you will be able to guide them to apply skills they *already* possess in more complex and demanding environments. This boils down to: add more strength here, loosen up there, be quicker, be slower and so on. Help your students re-define their sensory "good riding" skills using creative exercises and timely reminders to escape Pandora's box!

TIPS ON WHEN TO INTRODUCE MORE DIFFICULT SKILLS:

When can Suzie start jumping? How long will it take before my husband starts running the barrels? Larry has his heart set on fox hunting this fall, do you think he'll be ready? These are just a few of the questions instructors receive from their clientele on the subject of progressing toward more difficult skills. *When* to introduce a new skill rests on: proper skill prerequisites satisfied, the proper conditions and student desire. Lets look at these three variables closer.

SKILL PREREQUISITES ARE THOSE *EASIER* SKILLS THAT *DIRECTLY* RELATE TO THE PREPARATION FOR A *PARTICULAR* MORE DIFFICULT SKILL. At the novice level of riding, being able to properly steer with a direct rein, *directly* relates to the *preparation* for combining a direct rein with the application of the outside indirect regulating rein. Whereas, the novice skill of keeping one's feet in their stirrups would probably *not* be on most instructor's list of a direct "prerequisite" for learning *about* the indirect "regulating" rein, at the novice level. Meanwhile, being able to keep one's feet in their stirrups at the novice level, does directly relate to seat stability and so on. Thus, skill prerequisites are those necessary building blocks that insure reasonable success for attempting a more difficult *new* (to the student) riding skill. More examples of skill prerequisites are: being able to stay balanced at a somewhat stronger trot/jog, *prior* to attempting the canter; being able to coordinate all the aids necessary to ask a horse to spin, first out of a walk *prior* to out of the sliding stop; being able to stay on a horse who jumps small (or flat) *prior* to one jumping over bigger obstacles or riding a horse who jumps "big"; etc.

PROPER CONDITIONS EQUALLY INFLUENCE THE SUCCESSFUL OUTCOME OF ATTEMPTING MORE DIFFICULT SKILLS. Specific to riding lessons, we should be careful to proceed onto more difficult skills when conditions will be supportive not hindering. "Conditions" include: weather, footing, facility needs, outside interference, equine readiness, and so on. For example; when a particular student you teach only has stadium jumps at their home, organization will be needed to school cross country jumps either by shipping to such a facility or constructing cross country jumps at home. Should you ship to a cross country facility and the fences are not suitable or what gets built at home is flimsy, the conditions are simply not suitable on that given day. Try again. However, if it is raining out and the footing has remained outstanding, the conditions have remained supportive. Respect the influence *improper* conditions can have on a "first" attempt at more difficult skills. Unsuccessful experiences take a toll. Partially unsuccessful experiences usually mean either the rider lacked certain necessary prerequisites or the conditions were only moderately supportive thus placing a strain on student success. Of these first two variables, conditions can be harder to predict as they often depend on the "day."

WHILE LISTED LAST, STUDENT DESIRE, MUST RANK *FIRST* IN TERMS OF IMPORTANCE. Like love, desire is a many splendor thing. Permission to try a more difficult skill is what an instructor can organize. The student possesses the desire....... or not. While desire can be cultivated, it does *come from* the student. For instructors, student desire is a healthy measure of commitment in the joint venture of progressing horseback riding skills. Sadly, sometimes a student may feel they have outgrown their instructor's ability to teach them certain more advanced skills and this limits their desire. If you suspect this is the case, encourage them to move onto another qualified instructor.... it is time for this student. Likewise, if you are stretching your boundaries of teaching certain more difficult skills and your student begins to lack confidence in your abilities, it may be time for a "graded: higher skills" instructor. The circumstance of instructors continuing on with this student is similar to the green horse/green rider issue. With careful nurturing, solid study on the instructor's part and patience on the student's, "green" instructors of a *particular* "skill grade" *also* enjoy new successes. This instructor has desire too!

TIPS ON HOW TO INTRODUCE MORE DIFFICULT SKILLS:

The student's desire to move onto more difficult skills should be your *first* assessment, followed by proper preparations in terms of prerequisites and supportive general conditions. Certainly a student who is itching to try a more difficult skill is vastly different than a student who is reluctant. To complicate this issue further, occasionally, the itchy student is a long way off from being ready, meanwhile, some reluctant students do not have a clear understanding of their capabilities. Lesson plans to introduce "more difficult skills" are structured in one of two approaches. Either a brief *"no error"* lesson plan is provided or *"repetitive practice"* is planned. Lets look at these two contrasting approaches individually.

PROVIDING FOR A BRIEF "NO ERROR" APPROACH, FACILITATES IMPORTANT EXPOSURE TO A MORE DIFFICULT RIDING SKILL. This avenue is ideal for a student who is leery of trying a particular skill or for a student who is moderately ready, yet needs a challenge. The "no error" approach is based on the instructor creating a roll of preparations during the lesson, then as an opportune moment emerges, the more difficult skill is attempted. With these strategic preparations created by the instructor, the result is usually quite successful. Should this first attempt turn out to be only moderately successful, the attempt is *treated* as a success. The student is praised for having gotten their feet wet. The "no error" approach is brief. This technique leaves the student motivated and exposed but not *skilled*.......yet. Careful consideration should be given to the eager student with this approach. They should *not* attempt to practice this new skill on their own. Before any student practices more advanced skills on their own, sufficient practice time *under instruction* needs to be accomplished to lay a foundation of minimum capabilities. The keen organization involved in creating the "no error" approach is the result of skillful teaching. However, bear in mind, this teaching technique also lacks substance. It is repetitive practice that builds a rider's abilities for achieving more difficult skills. When the "no error" approach is used, it should be considered an introduction and a stepping stone toward repetitive practice.

PROVIDING FOR REPETITIVE PRACTICE BUILDS A RIDER'S SKILLS; HOWEVER, NOT ALL PRACTICE WILL BE SUCCESSFUL. Whether initially or following a "no error" introduction, repetitive practice is needed to cultivate and advance a student's abilities with respect to a more difficult riding skill. Unlike the "no error" approach, repetitive practice is *not* highly engineered by the instructor. Proper skill prerequisites and supportive conditions guarantee moderate or at least intermittent success for the student. The repetitive practice approach results in peaks and valleys which are healthy for learning. Lesson plans need to provide adequate time for this pendulum to swing both ways. Not only will the student learn from their successful attempts, but their less successful practice provides useful information to identify the components of success and failure. A rider's education that has included repetitive practice is sound and leads to independence.

REPETITIVE PRACTICE MEANS: REPETITIONS IN CLOSE SUCCESSION. REPETITIVE PRACTICE IS CEASED OR A RESTING BREAK IS GIVEN *JUST PRIOR* TO THE STUDENT TIRING. It is the opportunity for the student to try a more advanced skill over and over which enables them to build their individual skills and discover those components which lead to failure. With this technique, the *student* builds the roll while the instructor provides performance feedback. For example, a rider is now trying a 10 meter circle at the canter. This rider is instructed to perform a 10 meter circle at the middle of all four walls of an arena. Initially, each circle is slightly different. Some egg like, some flat on one side, some too big while every once in a while, one circle is *perfect*. Steadily, the repetitive practice increases the student's knowledge and physical coordination of aids and *more* circles become round and 10 meters in size. Once a students stops repetitive practice for a rest break or until another lesson, some decline of achievement can be expected. But, as a student repeats practice the same level of achievement comes more easily plus more strides forward!

Chapter Nine

STUDENT NEEDS & DESIRES

A goal is the end point aimed for.
Objectives are those means by which we intend to obtain the goal.

Take for example, John wants to participate in Fox Hunting. Thus, Fox Hunting is the goal. To design objectives to reach this goal, an instructor needs to identify areas of achievement that *are* measurable and will lead the student toward achieving their goal. Each objective should identify:
1) *the prevailing conditions* 2) *the skill and/or knowledge to be accomplished* 3) *to what measurable degree this skill and/or knowledge will be accomplished.* Back to John. John has been competently jumping up to three foot for a year now, however, all in a flat, sand ring. An example of a student performance objective for John to achieve prior to Fox Hunting is:

In a field with varied terrain (#1),
John will be able to jump up to three feet out of trot or canter (#2),
without hitting his horse in the mouth or the back (#3).

There will be a number of other objectives John will need to achieve in preparing for Fox Hunting, such as: riding in a large group of horses; being able to get on and off his horse without assistance; and so on. Objectives may or may not coincide with individual lesson plans. Most often, objectives can frequently be accomplished in a varying order.

82

Today, goals and objectives for horseback riding instruction yield to student and instructor determination rather equally. This is due to the artistic, sport and leisure profile of current day horseback riding activities. Years ago, determination of goals and thus objectives were mostly instructor driven. There were day to day needs centered around horsemanship, riding and driving. For the last century, most of the world's daily life and commerce has shifted steadily away from dependence on horses, to other forms of transportation. One hundred years ago, a household study of horsemanship, riding and driving would have closely resembled a household study of automobiles and/or computers today. In a short hundred years, the equestrian world has shifted to somewhat of a novelty. Will an equestrian newcomer still be riding horses in five years or even in three? For a vast majority of students new to horseback riding, this is not a probability in our modern world. Pressures *do* exist for instructors to design objectives that will enable a student to reach high goals quickly and cheaply. Thus, instructors are faced with how to say "no" to inappropriate demands, *tactfully*. Furthermore, there is an increased attitude that students are just as much a "client" as a student in *all* areas of education. Frequently this impacts the teaching - learning process in negative ways. Thorough planning of appropriate goals and objectives minimizes these negative pressures. Here are three important facets for tailoring goals and objectives:

REGULARLY, DETERMINE YOUR STUDENT'S *ABILITY* IN TERMS OF TIME FRAMES AND TIME MANAGEMENT. In the past, a goal determined the time frame for learning. Very often now, the time frame (time availability really) is set first by the student, and goals have to follow. Another words, our students tend to purchase what they can afford in terms of "time." This difference makes planning more difficult for instructors. Most of us teaching today, started out with goals leading the structure. Thus, *regular* affirmation of time availability is necessary for setting realistic goals.

INDIVIDUALIZE YOUR GOALS AND OBJECTIVES FOR *EACH* STUDENT. The vast majority of instruction occurs in group lessons. Tailoring goals and objectives right down to each individual rider, even for group lessons, results in better quality instruction.

SHARE YOUR OBJECTIVES FOR REACHING A GOAL *WITH* YOUR STUDENT/S. This is not privileged information. For most goals, several different schemes of objectives could be created; *all* resulting in a successful outcome. Thus, sharing *your* design of objectives with your student/s, lessens the risk of unexpected problems. Communicating with your student/s enables you to determine the suitability of your plans, plus prepares your student for meaningful learning. A tailored plan of goals and objectives, can only be achieved through thorough communication with your student/s.

TIPS TO RECOGNIZE AND RESOLVE BARRIERS TO LEARNING:

Barriers to learning are conditions that prevent your horseback riders from progressing at a normal rate. Within the individual lessons you teach, these barriers to learning cause your riders to progress slower than you expected and often result in some frustration or confusion for the student. Naturally the student's lifestyle outside your lessons can be a source of barriers to learning, however, let us focus on those barriers within riding lessons. Let us examine four primary areas: 1) inappropriate attention 2) false confidence 3) fear and nervousness 4) over facing and over load.

A FEW EXAMPLES OF INAPPROPRIATE ATTENTION ARE: DISTRACTIONS, LACK OF ATTENTION AND FOCUSING ON AREAS ASIDE FROM THE LESSON. To achieve appropriate attention, get your students more *involved* with their lesson. Plan and use activities that will require the rider's participation both physically and mentally. For example, at the conclusion of a group dressage lesson, ask your students to compose an original dressage test they will perform during their lesson next week. Then, the following week as they perform their dressage tests, assign each class member watching, a different facet to critique: "Karen - at the conclusion of Sam's test, I want you to critique his creativity; Lucy - look for how properly Sam's figures were executed; George, evaluate how correctly Sam used his aids to ride his test. Thus, *each* student has an individual job to do. *Each* student gets your individual feedback on their participation. Using activities that ask your students to *apply* their knowledge and skills reduces inappropriate attention.

FALSE CONFIDENCE IS A BARRIER TO LEARNING BECAUSE THE STUDENT BECOMES LAZY AND LESS DETAILED ABOUT THEIR LEARNING. These students have exaggerated opinions of their knowledge and skills. Tactfully, an instructor needs to allow the student to experience their skill and knowledge shortcomings *without* compromising safety. For example: Susie feels she has mastered sitting the trot, however, her horse has a relatively flat gait. Furthermore, her horse is quite tolerant and ignores some of Susie's stiffness; unfortunately this serves to nurse along Susie's false confidence. During a lesson on transitions that involves switching horses, her instructor indirectly addresses this issue by switching Susie to a bouncier horse. "Oh my goodness..... this horse has more spring........ gee this is hard to sit" expresses Susie. Increasing Susie's awareness of how much more there is to learn is a solid first step to dispel her false confidence.

FEAR AND NERVOUSNESS CAN BE EXTREME BARRIERS TO LEARNING. Blatant fears or nervousness such as afraid to ride following a serious fall, or nervous about making the same mistake *again*, are easy to identify. Overcoming fears and nervousness take confidence building. Less blatant fears and nervousness can be harder to detect. Is an excessively tense rider nervous or simply needs to stretch before they ride? Is a rider who has reluctance to use their crop, afraid of hurting the horse, or simply can't reach the hip of the horse? Sorting out fears and nervousness from other barriers to learning takes *thorough* communication and patience.

OVER FACING A STUDENT RESULTS IN FAILURE AND UNDERMINES CONFIDENCE. Heidi doesn't feel ready to trot; Henry tried to canter but could not keep his balance. Likewise, over loading a student results in confusion and failure. When a student has been over loaded, they have *too much* to manage to be successful. If your student takes a long time to answer a question, or their response comes too quickly and off base, these are signs of over load. In these cases, reduce the theory or tasks you are asking the student to accomplish... learning *is* after all on the student's clock, not ours.

TIPS TO DEAL WITH FEAR AND BUILD RIDER CONFIDENCE:

Let us divide fear into two aspects. Fear that the student acknowledges and fear that the body expresses. Fear that the student acknowledges are those conditions that a student accepts as something to be afraid of. Such as: fear of falling off, fear of failure, or even fear of the unknown. Whereas fear the body expresses, reveals the insecurities of the rider's seat, such as: clutching the reins for balance or fetal position to stay with a bouncy trot. Riders often are unaware of "body fear" because a rider's body fear is natural and may even feel helpful. In dealing with either type of fear or a combination thereof, positive experiences are necessary to build confidence. Let us look at how we can build confidence and lessen fear.

WHEN A STUDENT IS AFRAID OF A CERTAIN RIDING ACTIVITY, BUILD THEIR FOUNDATION SKILLS TO EXCEED THE NEEDS OF THAT ACTIVITY, PRIOR TO HAVING THEM TRY THE ACTIVITY THEY FEAR. IN A NUTSHELL, OVER PREPARE THE STUDENT. Examples of this would be: *for a rider afraid of jumping* - over develop the rider's strength and balance in the 2-point position *before* starting them over fences; *for a rider afraid to canter* - teach them how to achieve their balance during lengthenings to the trot and during the transitions to and from lengthening *prior* to their attempting the first canter; *for a rider afraid of riding in an open field* - have them master emergency control tactics such as circling or a pulley rein *before* going from the ring to an open field. By over preparing a student, you have given them room for minor errors plus helped them establish a higher sense of confidence prior to their initial try. These additional skills and confidence will increase the likelihood for a successful initial experience. Success changes fear into accomplishment. But should a student be fearful based on a previous *unsuccessful* experience, the same measures are helpful, however, it is imperative to seek a *student* paced decision on "when" the time has come to try the activity again. This creates commitment on the student's part and will let you know when they truly have the courage to risk another failure. Certainly many forms of motivation may be used by the instructor to persuade a student to try again when they seem ready, but in the end - following a previous failure, be sure the student has paced the decision to proceed.

TO REDUCE BODY FEAR, PHYSICALLY SUPPORT, DON'T CHALLENGE. PUT THE RIDER IN AS RELAXED AND COMFORTABLE A LEARNING ENVIRONMENT AS POSSIBLE. IN A NUTSHELL, DEVISE STEPPING STONES FOR YOUR STUDENTS. Examples of this would be: improving the fit of the saddle to the rider - this supports the proper position rather than the rider needing to over come the saddle too; putting a student on a lunge line with reins - enables the instructor to assist the student with steering but not necessarily do *all* the steering; using trot poles to maintain the trot rhythm up to a jump for a horse who tends to rush - enables the rider to work on themselves more and the horse's problems less; having your student ride a better trained western pleasure horse to feel proper neck reining - results in all the rider's aids blending because of the responsiveness of the horse. These teaching strategies provide "support" for the student's learning on a physical basis. In time, stepping stones gradually transform fearful instinctive body postures into secure riding skills. As new skills develop, body fear diminishes. When your student has become more secure and accomplished, begin to test their new skills. They are now ready for physical challenges.

TIPS FOR HELPING STUDENTS OVER LEARNING PLATEAUS:

While learning to ride follows a relatively standard progression of skills, this progression does not follow a standardized clock. When a *new* skill or concept *"clicks"* a learning plateau has ended and the student experiences a sense of accomplishment and motivation. On the other hand, learning plateaus that develop into learning slumps, create discouragement and even frustration for students and instructors alike. The instructor who helps a student cope with a particular learning slump is well on the way to helping their student hurdle that slump. Assisting each *individual* student over learning plateaus and slumps is the artist side of teaching horseback riding. Finding ways to minimize *commonly seen* learning slumps is the science side of teaching horseback riding. Lets look at some important points about helping our students to overcome slumps yet learn from plateaus.

LEARNING PLATEAUS ARE *AN OPPORTUNITY* TO PERFECT EXISTING SKILLS. Lets say we are walking ..... or running up a steep hill. When we get to the top, we welcome the flat plateau; this plateau allows us to catch our breath. Likewise, for learning complex horseback riding skills, learning plateaus *allow* riders to spend time on perfecting existing skills. Skill overload occurs when riders haven't had the opportunity to perfect existing skills before climbing the next steep hill. In a nutshell, your rider's body has run "out of breath." Some signs of skill overload are: physical reflexes that are too slow to organize for more advanced activities; a lack of ability to coordinate several tasks simultaneously; initial physical responses which are incorrect, yet corrected during practice. These situations translated into horseback riding language are: those riders who are folding and unfolding quite slowly while jumping a single jump will not be able to fold and unfold quickly enough between two fences set only one stride apart (physical responses that are too slow to organize for more advanced jumping); a rider who cannot steer and post at the same time (a lack of ability to coordinate several tasks simultaneously); a rider who comes up on the incorrect diagonal but after a few strides of trotting can feel the incorrect diagonal and fixes it (an initial physical response which is incorrect but corrected during practice). When skill overload occurs, the rider is not ready or prepared *for* that next steep hill; back up and perfect their existing skills; let the student catch their breath on learning plateaus.

THERE IS A NATURAL "READINESS" IN EACH LEARNER FOR MOVING ONTO THE NEXT STEP. Aside from prerequisite skills needed for more advanced activities, there also rests a natural "readiness" in each learner. This phenomenon becomes apparent when an instructor thinks a rider is ready for a more advanced skill, yet things fall apart when it is attempted. Individual student "readiness" is an intricate combination of preparation, confidence, aptitude and desire. Unfortunately learning slumps can lure riders and instructors alike, into proceeding toward more advanced skills, *before* the rider is truly ready. While instructors should develop a standard clock of time it takes for specific skills to be accomplished, some students will not progress at that "normal" rate of speed (slower or faster). Various aspects and elements of student "readiness" cannot be influenced by an instructor; they *are* student paced.

Helping students learn from plateaus and hurdle slumps takes patience and creativity. Most likely, when you know a student is benefiting from their current learning plateau, you have observed and helped numerous other students navigate and transition *on* from that plateau before. While your student may *want* to proceed, you know what is best: *not yet.* But when it comes to learning *slumps*, things get a lot more complicated and gray. The student is stuck and so are you. Generally both the student and the instructor have participated in this process *because* both *are* trying to hurdle the slump. With your student's permission, it is time to start some "experimental" remedies; try new/different resolutions to search for an answer to the student's problem; good luck!

TIPS FOR OVERCOMING "OLD BAD HABITS":

Instructors and students alike, moan over the challenging issue of "old bad habits." While these habits are unfortunate and often nagging, bad habits can be conquered with persistence and determination. A rule of thumb for overcoming an old bad habit is:

Achieve the proper execution of the horseback riding skill, twice as long as it has been performed improperly, and the student will be well on their way to overcoming their bad habit.

Usually, old bad riding habits aren't perverse, just incorrect enough, that the rider can manage with the improper skill *until* new skills are attempted. Adding new skills creates a complex environment. Again the old bad habit strikes. Bad habits weaken a rider's foundation of seat, skill and judgment. Even more paradox, "old bad habits" tend to *feel* natural to the student. Because slightly incorrect horseback riding skills are easily overlooked, the result is a sub-standard degree of performance *naturalized*. Sports researchers consider a skill to be naturalized when little or no conscious thought is needed to perform that skill, that way. An *undesirable* habit naturalized, requires undivided attention during practice to reverse. Down the road of practice, less concentration will be needed, but the road is long, repetitious, and potentially monotonous. Horseback riding instructors need to be patient, supportive and ready to lend a shoulder as students embark on the mileage necessary to reverse old bad habits. Meanwhile, the student has to be ready emotionally and physically to embark on this task.

AS A STUDENT GRASPS THE *CORRECTED SKILL* THEY NEED TO NATURALIZE, REDUCE YOUR STEP BY STEP INSTRUCTION. Put yourself in the ring setting. John has a bad habit of sitting too far back on Trigger going up steep grades. While John is comfortable in this position, John's weight, taxes Trigger's loins. Furthermore, Trigger is also relatively unresponsive to John's steering aids when he sits in this position. After several lessons to address this problem, John has begun to grasp the feel of the correct position riding up hills. On his own, he begins to correct his balance from *his* sense of feel, *not from instruction*. Now, shift your instruction to emphasize the improvements gained in the responsiveness of the horse. All rider equitation improvements result in a more responsive horse to the rider's aids. This fact can certainly be a selling point to a student for the need to change an old bad habit. However, the occurrence of this dimension generally, does not become clear *to the student*, until the student can feel their changed habit correlate with their horse's changed behavior. While horses take note and respond to improved equitation, unfortunately, the change might be ever so slight. This means the initial improvements yielded by the some horses, frequently go unnoticed by a rider struggling to change a bad habit. As a student displays the ability to correct their seat based on their feel and are able to coordinate these corrections in a timely manner, the horse's responsiveness also becomes greater. More and more, the horse's improved responsiveness will be clear to the rider. These accomplishments help to build motivation *and* reward the rider for their transformation; both horse and rider benefit.

AND FINALLY, AS A RIDER CAN FREELY EMBARK ON LEARNING NEW SKILLS WITH *LITTLE* RELAPSE OF THEIR "OLD BAD HABIT", THEY ARE NEARING THE *NATURALIZATION* OF THE DESIRED RIDING SKILL. Let us check back with John. His practice of catching up in his balance with Trigger going up hills is improving. Not only does Trigger steer more easily, but John can also attempt to perform transitions from one gait to another on the slope without a loss of his improved balance.

When (and if) John relapses more than a "little" while attempting new skills, return for additional concentrated practice solely on his sitting forward with the horse going up hills. However, when John is close to success with only *minute* relapses, these attempts should be treated as a successful milestones toward the permanent conquering of the bad habit. In short order he *will* naturalize the desired skill, thus breaking free from that "old bad habit!" *Congratulations!* Riders who *naturalize* equitation improvements, prove new additional skills are easier to learn, over and over again.

TIPS FOR INCREASING STUDENT MOTIVATION:

Most students have periods of higher and lower motivation. Occasionally there are students that need constant motivating. Luckily, horseback riding students are *generally* highly motivated due to their love for the horse but nonetheless these students are *still* subject to motivational peaks and valleys. Lets look at some ways we can help students through those valley days.

STUDENTS WHO FREQUENTLY EXPERIENCE FATIGUE WHEN RIDING, *LOOSE* MOTIVATION. When lack of motivation is connected to physical fatigue, select exercises and activities which require less energy and examine if strength building exercises, better nutrition or more sleep are needed by your student. Put yourself in the ring setting. Henry has suffered from an *obvious* performance decline during your last four lessons. Where he usually does not have problems cantering for five minutes, he now needs frequent breaks to rest. Furthermore, Henry just seems a bit "blue" about riding in general. As you seek the root of this problem, you determine that he has been studying hard for mid-terms at school. Henry has been operating on *little* sleep for the last several weeks. In his case, focusing your current lesson plans to progress his theoretical knowledge and providing him quality demonstrations in lieu of excessive sweat producing riding time for Henry, is just plain common sense. That is until *after* mid-term!

STUDENTS WHO ARE BORED, *LOOSE* MOTIVATION. Perhaps the most challenging student an instructor can have is a bored student. These lessons often result in a *tired instructor* who tries to "impart" enthusiasm and motivation. Additionally, bored students often present distractions to the ring setting which challenge class control. Key to increasing the motivation of a bored student is building upon activities *they* choose. Student chosen topics for lesson plans become vital for bored students. While these students often choose activities they are not ready for, negotiating with these students to arrive at a workable compromise helps to increase their motivation. For example: Alex is in a group lesson of six. These students are learning how to run barrels. So far, they have been walking, jogging and cantering the barrels to learn the cloverleaf pattern. The dynamics of swinging too far out (which looses time) and cutting in too sharply (which knocks over a barrel) are getting conquered. But, Alex is *bored*. She wants to RUN the barrels! Her instructor addresses the situation at the beginning of a lesson: "Alex, it seems to me you are bored with our preparations *for working up to* running barrels; what would you like to do today?" Naturally, Alex responds: "I think we should be given a chance to RUN the barrels." Her instructor responds with a compromise: "While this group is not quite ready to *run* the entire pattern, you *are* ready to run parts of the pattern. Start with running to your first barrel, setting up and getting around that barrel then returning to a trot to finish. Eventually we will progress to running more of the pattern as you can maintain sufficient control." Alex is satisfied with this compromise; the class proceeds.

STUDENTS WHO ARE CONFUSED CAN LOOSE MOTIVATION. Student involvement is a fundamental factor for meaningful learning to take place. While a slight degree of confusion can motivate a student to catch up; a student who *remains* confused is in danger of loosing motivation *not only* for what is being taught, but for horsemanship and/or riding in general. Teaching above a student's level of ability has costly results. This holds true for cognitive *and* psychomotor learning. While creative teaching includes challenging students, careful consideration of students' current knowledge and skills is fundamental. Confused students are in danger of *failing* which mostly decreases motivation. While physical safety concerns are most often cited as the reason *why* teachers should adhere to *levels of instruction* for sports education; two other equally important reasons exist: motivation and learning opportunities...... perhaps a different *kind* of safety! Keeping riding instruction *within* the reach of the student *increases* motivation.

TIPS TO "SOBER" EXCESS MOTIVATION:

Let us examine a student's enthusiasm which rolls into a dangerous degree of glee. Let us call this: *excess motivation*. Instructors do not fuel excess motivation, but we can be guilty of failing to recognize its beginning stages. Instructors who have a case of student excess motivation, are faced with *when* and *how* to sober this barrier to learning. Contributing factors are: ignorance, youth, overt competitive tendencies, peer pressure and so on. Ramifications are: safety problems, lack of learning basics, goal orientation excluding the horse's well-being, and so on. Truthfully, at first, excess motivation can seem - "o.k." Unfortunately, excess motivation is just that: excess. The mood where meaningful learning occurs, has been lost. Hence this dictates when to apply measures to "sober" this motivation. Horseback riding instructors need to make this value judgment, the same as instructors of other studies. Applying, "sobering" measures are a responsibility of quality instruction. Lessons which reduce this excess motivation are based on upholding the values and principles of horsemanship we cherish.

TALE TELL SIGNS OF EXCESS MOTIVATION USUALLY BEGIN WITH A DISREGARD FOR INSTRUCTION ON THE HEELS OF PERSONAL SUCCESS OR PERSONAL FAILURE. Often the disregard for instruction can be so subtle, that we initially miss this warning sign. Example #1: Kenny has been getting his canter leads almost every time. Once he became more disciplined about using his leg aids properly and chose a timing where the horse was properly balanced for the lead, his canter lead problems disappeared. Riding high on this success did go to Kenny's head. He began to inquire about moving onto flying changes and other substantially advanced exercises. Later his inquires became a full fledge insistence to be *"allowed"* to learn these skills. Example #2: Roberta fell off her horse several times. In both instances, she lost her lateral balance and was unable to stay on her horse's playfulness. Being a high achiever, she was not willing to let these failures do anything but motivate her. She signed up for extra lessons. Actually, she signed up for three times the amount of riding, prior to falling off. And last, she practically demanded to continue riding the horse she had fallen off of. Several weeks went by and she had a very close encounter with falling off again. What is evident in both of these scenarios? Both Kenny and Roberta are becoming difficult to teach because of their *excess* motivation.

IDEALLY, ANTIDOTES FOR EXCESS MOTIVATION WILL SIMPLY REDUCE THE STUDENT'S MOTIVATION TO A HEALTHIER LEVEL. It is mostly the reality of increasing consequence which settles excess motivation. Let us return to our two examples. Once Kenny realizes he is not ready for flying changes his enthusiasm will be more appropriately geared toward getting ready for flying changes sometime in the future. An example antidote for Kenny's situation is: invite him to audit a class *he* feels is substantially more advanced. Meanwhile, *this* class *is* getting ready for flying changes; they have ten lessons scheduled to prepare them for starting flying changes and this is their first preparation lesson. Kenny is welcome to audit all of these preparation lessons and their later lessons of learning, and doing flying changes. An example antidote for Roberta's situation is: announce a special activity for Roberta's next riding lesson. Her class will be video taped for the first time. After riding, this class will then go to their tack room to review the video tape. First, the students are allowed to watch themselves riding. Then the students are presented with an activity. Select footage of a more advanced student doing the same riding exercises, is shown to this class. Each student is asked to compare their lateral balance to that of the more advanced student. Then a discussion is encouraged by the instructor on ways to achieve better lateral balance. The instructor asks the students to distill three primary ways their lateral balance should improve; *as a class*. From this activity, Roberta begins to realize more quantity of riding may not resolve her balance problems; however, increased concentration on her collapsed hip which affects her lateral balance will probably help her stay in the saddle more. Of the many tasks instructors face in teaching horseback riding, reducing *excess* motivation to a level where meaningful learning takes place requires a combination of rules and compassion.

TIPS FOR TEACHING "RUSTY" STUDENTS:

"Rusty" students generally fall into three categories. They are:

- *Regular students, whom for one reason or another, have not ridden for a short period of time*
- *Students who are returning to riding, following an extended period of time*
- *Riders who have been riding regularly; however, have not been under instruction for a period of time*

These three conditions are quite different. These three categories are being presented in the order of probability with which an instructor will encounter them. Now, let us look at these three categories closely.

REGULAR STUDENTS, WHOM FOR ONE REASON OR ANOTHER, HAVE NOT RIDDEN FOR A SHORT PERIOD OF TIME. For the purposes of time delineation, let us consider this category to be those periods away from riding that range three months to a year. Generally, for a student to be "rusty", more than a few days have been missed. This occurrence is common with teenagers who want to participate in a different sport for a season or working individuals very busy with work requiring horseback riding to take a back seat for a short period or a marriage, a pregnancy and so on. While these riders have not forgotten what they have learned, they *have* lost general fitness *for* horseback riding. A lack of horseback riding, mostly affects fitness and the rider's ability to coordinate complex skills. Therefore, a student returning to riding following a short break, should first focus on rebuilding their horseback riding muscles and stamina previously enjoyed. Initially, avoid complex skills for this returning rider. During private instruction, this is easy to custom design. But for a student who participates in group instruction, consider temporarily placing this returning student in a class *one level* below their previous abilities. This strategy has two benefits. First, the lower class's slower pace and more elementary exercises enables a returning rider to *focus* on developing riding fitness. Secondly, the returning rider can provide quality demonstrations for introducing more advanced skills to this lower level class. Fun for the returning student; inspiring for the lower level class. Meanwhile, a student who goes directly into their previous class level will be more subjected to their "rustiness." Carefully start this student with simple exercises of short duration and fewer repetitions than the rest of their class. Interestingly, humans loose muscle fitness *more quickly* than horses. So, if they are riding their own horse, the horse *is* more fit than the student.

STUDENTS WHO ARE RETURNING TO RIDING, FOLLOWING AN EXTENDED PERIOD OF TIME: TEND TO BE "RUSTY" IN MORE WAYS THAN FITNESS. These riders frequently have forgotten how to perform some of the skills they once were able to do with reasonable ease. "Forgetting" is not select to the aging process but also influenced by the *use* of a skill. Therefore, lengthy time away, contributes to "forgetting." While these riders once rode at a certain skill level, the likelihood that they will be able to pick up where they left off is rare. Ease of balancing, timing of aids, perception which influences decision making are all affected by extended periods away from riding. Oddly enough, riders who have missed extended periods of riding time tend to "perceive" their rustiness more accurately than riders who have not ridden for shorter periods. Therefore, care needs to be taken by the instructor to gently address this issue. Respect that these riders *are* returning to horseback riding, and carefully explore what class level best fits these riders. Helpful are: assessment lessons; encouraging auditing of other lessons; periodic progress reviews; and so on.

RIDERS WHO HAVE BEEN RIDING REGULARLY; HOWEVER, HAVE NOT BEEN UNDER INSTRUCTION FOR A PERIOD OF TIME. These riders are "rusty" in terms of *taking* instruction. For children, a lack of attention is often the by-product; for adults, a tug of war on lesson planning tends to occur; after all, this horseback rider has been creating their own lesson plans for some time. Patience and leadership are strengths an instructor needs to draw upon. Helpful are: *shared* decision making on lesson plans; emphasis on *future* goals; incorporating *teamwork* exercises with other students; requesting detailed student *critiques* following lessons; and so on.

TIPS FOR SAYING GOOD-BYE:

Some good-byes are temporary, such as a teen going off to college, a pregnancy, dwindling finances and so on. Other good-byes are permanent such as a move, a student's decision to change instructors, an instructor retiring from teaching horseback riding, a student deciding to quit horseback riding and so on. Good-byes are usually a transition involving mixed emotions. On the bright side, the chance to say good-bye is generally heart warming. In some circumstances, a good-bye may represent an incremental progress award given from instructor to student, of: "it is time for you to progress *to* a higher level instructor." On the other hand, some good-byes are an instructor's best effort of opening a door for a student during times of difficulty. While saying good-bye is a personal and novel situation each time, here are some thoughts to consider for saying good-bye to a student of your horseback riding instruction.

AIDE ALL STUDENTS DURING GOOD-BYE TRANSITIONS. Making an effort to aide each student during a "good-bye" *is* worthwhile. Most students readily appreciate and prefer their instructor's assistance with many of the related decisions of this transition. While most good-byes are some form of a student "spreading their wings"; nonetheless, this transition can create turmoil for students. Develop a system to help students during this transition time. Your personal system will create helpful expectations upon which a student can rely. For example: some barns give "going away" parties, while other riding schools choose to honor their departing students with a memento gift. One creative horseback riding school developed a school policy that when a student was leaving, this student was given a portfolio of essays written by their fellow students titled: *Our Favorite Memory - a Remember When? Portfolio*. This collection was presented to the departing student at the conclusion of their last lesson, together with the addressees, e-mail & telephone numbers of their horseback riding friends. Additionally, helping a student to feel welcome when or if they should they decide to return, goes a long way to win hearts.

GOOD-BYES, EITHER TEMPORARY OR PERMANENT, OFTEN INCLUDE A SAD GOOD-BYE TO THE STUDENT'S MOUNT. While saying good-bye between humans can be hard enough, many good-byes in horseback riding instruction also involve a special horse. The bonds between horses and human grows deep. Providing adequate personal time for this student to also say their good-bye to this special horse will go a long way. Furthermore, ideas such as providing an instant camera to this student so they can take some "good-bye" pictures, or selecting a photo of this horse from your personal collection is a thoughtful gesture. Some instructors write "how are you doing" letters several weeks following a student's departure, indirectly "penned" by this special horse, which includes newsy information on how things are at the riding school, from the horse's perspective. Adults and children alike, enjoy hearing from a horse special to them.

BE SURE TO SETTLE TROUBLES OF STUDENT/INSTRUCTOR ROLES PRIOR TO THE FORTHCOMING TRANSITION. While most good-byes are a natural part of anticipated planning, some are not. Thus, it is difficult to say "good-bye" to a student when troubles between a student and an instructor have not been resolved. In the hope and prayer of a better future day, most horseback riding instructors plan with a long look down the road when it comes to role conflict. However, when a transition *is* at hand, this long look down the road changes. It is best to settle pending troubles as a part of a "good-bye"; not following a "good-bye." This means *addressing* communication problems and mis-understandings, *clarifying* previous discipline measures, or *verifying* the reason why Roberta has not yet gained the opportunity to ride High-Ho Silver.

FOLLOWING A GOOD-BYE TO A STUDENT, WHOM IS OFF TO "SPREAD THEIR WINGS", CONCLUDE WITH HELPING THEIR FRIENDS ADJUST. *Both* humans and horses *miss* valued friends. Your job will not be complete until you have also eased their sense of loss. Lending an ear, an occasional hug, and/or the creation of new activities to help the time pass more easily are a good start. Thankfully, these measures help instructors too!

BIOGRAPHY of JO A. STRUBY

Jo holds a M.A. in Education with an emphasis in Equestrian Studies (1986) and a B.S. in Equestrian Studies with a minor in Education (1986-graduating magna cum laude). Both of her academic degrees are from Salem International University, West Virginia. She also holds a Riding Master Diploma, 1975 from Meredith Manor School of Horsemanship where she was named to the Who's Who List for Outstanding Students in American Vocational and Technical Schools, 1975.

As an administrator, Jo was formerly Dean of Meredith Manor School of Horsemanship, 1980-1985. She has a strong professional background in teacher education, program administration and curriculum development. While teaching at this internationally known school for 10 years, she focused on the development of the jumping and teaching departments.

As former Vice-President for the United States Combined Training Association, Jo served on the executive committee from 1987-1989 and the board of governors from 1984-1989. During her tenure, she developed the AHSA-USCTA Combined Training Officials seminars as well as carried out the educational seminars for the general membership including beginning the USCTA Event Colleges. In 1988 she received the USCTA's Governor's Cup Award for outstanding contributions to the sport of Eventing.

As an educator, Jo has provided equestrian education to riders and instructors, nationally, since 1975. From 1989 through 2002 she provided an on-going education program for horseback riding instructors focusing on improving their teaching effectiveness. She has also developed a working student program for Shenandoah Farm of Staunton, Virginia on training and breeding, and advised Wetherbee Farm of Boxboro Massachusetts on developing their Fitness by Riding Program.

As a rider, competitor and athlete, Jo has trained and competed through the Advanced Level in Eventing and the Prix St. Georges Level in Dressage.

She earned her USDF Bronze and Silver Medal Rider Awards during the late 1970's. She has also been long listed during the 1980's for The Eventing Olympic Team.

INDEX

A

B

Fox Hunters
    lesson examples of, 15, 82

G

Goals
    priorities - listing of, 60, 61
    student, 13, 14, 51, 52, 82, 83
Good-byes, 93, 94
Green horses & advanced riders, 11
Green riders & horses, 7, 8, 11, 12, 79
Group lessons
    structure of, 19, 20, 21, 22, 23, 27, 28
    student dialogue during, 22, 25, 52, 53

H

Homework
    assigning, 29, 30, 31
    related to theory, 29, 30 ,31, 32, 33
Horsemanship
    horses' participation, 7, 8
    safety standards for, 1, 2, 34, 35
    teaching, 3, 4, 7, 8, 83
Horses
    assisting in teaching, 7, 8, 47, 48
    balance of, 49, 50
    body awareness of, 7, 8, 75, 76, 77
    comfort of, 7, 8, 69, 70, 92
    green, 8, 11, 12
    movement of, 75, 76, 77
    observational learning of, 10, 11, 21
    schooled, finding, 8, 9, 10
    schooled, learning from, 8, 9, 10, 11, 12
    schooled, making, 10, 11
    sour, 11
Horse's names, 2, 7, 15, 29, 37, 43, 94
Hunters / Jumpers
    lesson examples of, 49, 50, 61, 67, 72,
       73, 74

I

Inappropriate attention, 84
Individual feedback
    from the instructor, 19, 20, 26
    from other students, 22
    with pictures, 61
    with video footage, 91
Independent
    riding, during lessons, 22, 23
    study, 31, 32, 33
Information overload, 25
Instruction
    demonstrations, 25
    feedback to student/s, 25, 42, 44, 45
    less structured, 17, 18, 27
    planning, 13, 14
    presenting, clearly, 38, 39
    progressing, 86, 87
        with sequencing steps, 16, 17
    proper conditions, 79
    prompting, 19, 50
    skill confirmation, 25
    step by step, 16, 17, 87, 88, 89
    student practice, 25, 44, 45, 70, 71
    tests, 41, 42, 44, 45, 55
    time frames of, 18, 31, 32, 33, 92, 93
    visual, 22, 25, 71
Instructor
    avoiding of, 17, 18
    burn-out, 18
    dependence, 19
    paced instruction, 16
Intermediate (middle level) lesson
    examples, 26, 27, 43, 45, 67, 72, 73
    structure of, 14, 15, 24, 25, 26, 27, 78,
        79, 87

J

Jumping
    lesson examples of, 61, 67, 72, 73, 74,
        78, 79, 86

K

Kinesthesia, 47, 71, 74, 75, 76, 77

L

Learning
  active; definition, 13, 14
  basics of, 24, 25, 26
  cognitive domain, 21, 22, 23, 24, 25,
      26, 45, 46
  curves, 71, 72, 73, 86, 87
  determining, 13, 14, 41, 42
  gaps, bridging, 61, 62, 63
  passive; definition, 13, 14
  plateaus, 30, 31, 61, 62, 63, 86, 87
  psychomotor domain, 90
Lecturing, 24, 25, 26, 30, 31, 32, 33
Less structured lessons, 17, 18
Lesson/s,
  advanced students, 3, 4, 5, 6, 7, 8, 14,
      15, 26, 27, 78
  beginner students, 3, 4, 5, 6, 7, 8, 27, 76
  goals/objectives, 82, 83
  group/s, 21, 22, 23, 92, 93
  intermediate students, 3, 4, 5, 6, 7, 8,
      45, 67
  lunging, 14, 41, 86
  music, 73
  planning, 13, 14
  presenting material, 38, 39
  semi-private, 20, 21
  time frames of, 18
  unmounted, 54
  weather concerns, 53, 54, 78, 79
  warm up period, 66, 67
  wrapping up, 27, 28, 67, 68, 69
Libraries
  of video footage, 64
  of written material, 31, 32, 33

M

Megaphones, etc, 38
Mental practice/rehearsal, 32, 57, 58, 59

S

Saddle
    fitting rider, 86
Saddleseat,
    lesson examples of, 68, 69
Safety
    and beginners, 16, 17
    checks of equipment, 34, 35
    concerns, 69, 70, 90, 91
    conducting checks, 34, 35
    nets, 69, 70
    teaching appliances of, 61, 62, 63
    with horsemanship, 52, 53
Saw horse, 36
School horses - finding, 8, 9, 10, 11
School masters, 8
Semi-private lessons
    structure of, 20, 21
    student dialogue during, 21, 25 ,26
Sensitivity - riders', 77, 78
Skill/s
    analogies of, 64, 65
    foundation, 73, 74, 85, 86, 87, 88, 89
    mastery, 27
    more difficult - how, 79, 80, 81
    more difficult - when, 78, 79
    overload of, 86, 87
    perfecting of, 52, 53
    prerequisities for, 13, 14, 15, 78, 79
Step by step instruction, 16, 17
Stretching
    the horse, 68, 75, 76
    the rider, 66, 67, 68, 69
Stirrup ties, 61
Students'
    anxiety at competitions, 56, 57
    bored, 50, 51, 52, 89, 90
    challenging, 52, 53, 55, 56
    clothes, 36, 37
    confusion, 90
    creativity, 61
    focus, 19, 20, 26
    goals, 51, 52, 82, 83
    horsemanship of, 4

needs, 19, 20 ,39
new - evaluating, 39, 40, 41
progress, 45, 49, 50
rusty, 92, 93
their senses, 73, 74
utilizing video, 63, 64
Summaries, verbal, 27, 28

T

Teacher Task Analysis, 24, 25
Teaching
    aids & tools, 56, 57, 75
    appliances, 61, 62, 63
    behaviors, 24, 25, 26
    giving compliments, 44, 45
    green horses & riders, 11, 12
    horsemanship, 3, 4
    in cold weather, 53, 54
    rider cool-down, 67, 68, 69
    rider warm-up, 66, 67
    saying goodbye, 93, 94
    time of, 30, 31
Terms
    choosing, 38, 39
    defining & redefining, 49, 50
    wording, 74
Tests, 15, 28, 41, 42, 44, 45, 55, 86
Theory, 29, 30, 31, 46, 54
    when to avoid, 54
Therapeutic riding, 67, 71
Trail riding/Gymkhana riding
    lesson examples of, 21, 45, 87, 88, 89
Training
    school horses, 8, 9, 10, 11

U

UUUU, every page of text

V

Video/s
  instructor development, 36, 42
  student reviews, 54, 91
  using, 63, 64
  "take home", 58, 59
  value of using, 24, 25, 36, 47, 48, 54,
      63, 64
Visual learning, 22, 71
Vocabulary, 49, 50
Voice, instructors', 37, 38

W

Western,
  lesson examples of, 16, 17, 47, 50, 57,
      78, 86, 89
Whips, 61, 62

the X, Y, Z 's are up to you!